The Knowledge

*Every Gun's guide
to conservation*

Game & Wildlife
CONSERVATION TRUST

First published in Great Britain in 2018 by
Game & Wildlife Conservation Trading Ltd
Burgate Manor, Fordingbridge SP6 1EF
www.gwct.org.uk

A catalogue record for this book is available from the
British Library.

First printed June 2018.

978-1-901369-30-4

Written by Jennifer Brewin and Joe Dimbleby.
Designed and typeset in FlareSidhe and Minion Pro
by James Swyer.

Front cover © Jon Farmer
(with thanks to William Powell)

Foreword

One can never have enough knowledge about the natural world. There are always new things to learn, both for beginners and 'old hands'. That knowledge is key to valuing and respecting our natural environment, and nurturing greater biodiversity and species abundance within it. This book represents a strong positive step towards reaffirming shooters' relationship with the game and wildlife they love.

When it comes to wild food, and associated flora and fauna, we have been left with a hugely valuable legacy in the UK. It would be a tragedy to lose this. As stewards of the landscape, avoiding such an outcome is our responsibility. Without an understanding of quarry species, their habitat, and management, shooters risk not only the loss of their sport, but also huge harm to conservation of UK species, and an ever-greater disconnection between society and the natural resources on which it depends. Those who kill and eat their own meat have a closer relationship to their food than those who go to the supermarket to purchase it – they value that food more, and the environment it came from.

No gun needs to demonstrate their competence to go out shooting today – but tomorrow they may well do. Any responsible shooter with a strong hunting ethic should be able to answer the questions in this book, and will feel closer to their natural surroundings – and get greater enjoyment out of their shooting – for reading it. I would encourage readers also to commit themselves to obtaining the GWCT's new accredited game shot certificate, and to continue expanding their knowledge in the years to come.

We owe it to ourselves and to the wider world to be the most responsible participants in the life of the countryside, and the securest custodians of its future. This starts with *The Knowledge*.

Ray Mears

© Woodlore

What this book is:

1. Filling the conservation gap in the existing shooting guide library.
2. To explain some of what goes on behind the scenes the rest of the year outside shoot days, and reveal the ways in which a gamekeeper is a working conservationist whose job involves much more than looking after gamebirds.
3. Focused on improving standards in released bird shooting and encouraging wild game management. Hence the Code of Good Shooting Practice (see p. 211 for details) is quoted throughout.
4. A guide for both experienced Shots and people starting out with no understanding of the background to shooting.
5. Designed to give **Guns the right questions to ask their own shoots or the ones they visit or buy days from** to discover the level of quality and encourage the change we all want to see. (example questions are included at the end of each chapter).
6. An introduction to wild grey partridge conservation as a key part of our preserving our shooting and countryside heritage and an indicator of the health of the farmland ecology.
7. A guide to some of the most controversial issues of the day affecting shooting, e.g. lead shot and use of medication in game rearing.
8. An account of the law relevant to a Gun's experience of a shoot day. Contrary to the idea that shooting is unregulated, it is governed by a vast amount of legislation covering every aspect of shoot management.

What this book is not:

1. A guide to improve your shooting technique, tell you what equipment you need or how a shooting day is structured. There are plenty of good guides out there that do that already.
2. A "how to" book. It won't teach you what to do, but rather to recognise good conservation work when you see it, and understand whether shoots are meeting the required standards.
3. A comprehensive guide to all forms of shotgun shooting.
4. A guide to rifle shooting, air rifle shooting, deer management or gundog training.

Become a GWCT Accredited Game Shot™

This publication also serves as the reference book for a new online voluntary assessment scheme designed to test shooters' knowledge.

This book and the accompanying test aim to improve your confidence and understanding in:

- Asking appropriate questions of their own shoots or the ones they visit or buy days from.
- Appreciating the ways in which a gamekeeper is a working conservationist.
- Engaging in controversial issues affecting shooting (e.g. lead shot and the use of medication in game rearing)
- Explaining the ways legislation and regulation covers shoot management.

The test will give you a score at the end plus areas for improvement and a certificate if you pass.

You can complete the assessment today and become a GWCT Accredited Game Shot™ at **www.gwctknowledge.com**

CONTENTS

© *Laurie Campbell*

1. Pheasants

Pheasants are the most numerous gamebirds in the UK, and the most common quarry for shooting. The possible impact of pheasant release on the environment is an important issue, and as driven pheasant shoots are widespread, the potential effect on the countryside from pheasant management is greater than that of other gamebirds. The GWCT has carried out a wealth of research into how pheasant shoots can be managed to maximise the environmental benefits and minimise the potential harms. Adhering to codes of practice and best practice guidelines is critical to responsible shoot management.

Why are pheasants released for shooting?

Gamebird releasing increased in the 20th century, largely in response to declines in wild grey partridges as farming modernised. Game management began to include rearing and releasing to provide the quarry needed. Although the grey partridge responded well to the more traditional gamekeeping methods, they were not as well suited to rear and release as the pheasant. According to the GWCT's National Gamebag Census, more than three quarters of birds released for shooting are pheasants while the remainder are mostly red-legged partridges. A small number of grey partridge are still released, either for conservation or for shooting. From the 1960s onwards, as rearing methods developed, the success of rear and release pheasant shoots grew. The vast majority of shoots now release birds, which are reared on game farms or rearing fields on the shoot itself. Completely wild bird shoots do exist but they are much rarer.

The Code of Good Shooting Practice states that shooting must not commence until the birds are mature and fully adapted to the wild – a minimum of one month from release. © David Mason

Where do released birds come from?

Pheasants and partridges are normally bought from a game farmer as eggs, day-old chicks or young birds, called poults. Pheasant poults are generally bought at 6-8 weeks old, and red-legged partridge at 11-13 weeks. The gamekeeper will either buy eggs and chicks and rear them on the shoot, or buy in poults ready to transfer to the release pen. Many eggs and chicks are purchased from Continental game farms, but in general most poults are bought from within the UK. Game farmers and gamekeepers must comply with the regulations relating to gamebird rearing and should abide by is the Code of Practice for the Welfare of Gamebirds Reared for Sporting Purposes. All UK game farms that are members of the Game Farmers Association (GFA) abide by the code, guaranteeing high welfare standards, but not all suppliers are part of the GFA.

How is it done?

When the pheasant poults reach 6-8 weeks of age they are moved to a shoot and placed in large, usually open-topped, release pens sited in suitable woodland, normally between June and August. Over the next 3-6 weeks the birds gradually disperse to use surrounding woodland and specifically planted game crop areas during the day, returning to the area around the pen to roost in trees at night. There are usually three to four months between release of the birds to the woodland pen and the start of shooting. Released pheasants are therefore around 6 months old at the start of the season. The timing of the release is aimed at ensuring that birds are mature and fully adapted to their environment by the time shooting commences in late October or early November. The Code of Good Shooting Practice states that shooting must not commence until the birds are mature and fully adapted to the wild – a minimum of one month from release.

Why are release pens used?

Pheasant release pens are usually situated in woodland, sometimes on the woodland edge, and range in size. Larger ones may be up to 10 hectare (16 football pitches), while smallest ones may be as little as a tenth of a hectare (the size of a penalty area). They provide a secure environment where the young birds can acclimatise to their new habitat. In particular, they give the birds the opportunity to adapt to roosting in the lower branches of trees, thus avoiding the attention of ground predators, especially foxes.

Do they roam freely when they are released?

Yes. Once they leave their release pens, pheasants are not confined to a particular area, tending to spend time during the day in game crops planted specifically to hold, shelter and feed them, then returning to woodland at night to roost. Often they return to the pen where they were released.

Did you know?

14% of total UK woodland area is managed for pheasant shooting. This is 28% in England, and 4% in Scotland and Wales.

Follow the Code

Replenishing birds mid-season
"Birds must never be released to replenish or replace any birds already released and shot in that season"

Buying British
"Shoot managers should support UK game producers as the preferred source of stock for release"

Replenishing birds mid-season

The practise of releasing birds after the start of the season to make up the numbers (sometimes called 'topping up') is a breach of the Code of Good Shooting Practice. It states that "Birds must never be released to replenish or replace any birds already released and shot in that season." The principal reason for this is that it does not allow them time to acclimatise to their surroundings, which is why the Code stipulates that shooting must not commence until one month from release. The ethos is that the birds should be adapted to their environment. Topping up may also lead to inappropriately high levels of shooting in one area, causing more disturbance to wildlife and potentially increasing the incidental shooting of wild gamebirds.

In addition to breaching the Code there are legal implications to topping up. It may put the shoot at risk of breaking the 2006 Animal Welfare Act. There are also restrictions on the time between medications being administered and livestock entering the food chain, which will infringe the Food Safety Act 1990.

Did you know?

GWCT calculations estimate that 43 million pheasants were released in 2012.

© David Mason

Shoots have a responsibility to care for remaining pheasants after the end of the season.
© *GWCT*

Pheasant release: environmental effects

What effect can the release of pheasants have on the local environment?

Positive effects are seen in the surrounding woodland and farmland as a result of management measures undertaken for the pheasants and which tend to benefit other wildlife as well. In general, any negative effects are seen around the release pen, feed sites and wherever birds congregate in large numbers, because of direct effect of the birds being present.

What are the positive effects?

Some of the measured positive effects include: 22-32% more songbirds in woods managed for pheasants[1]; many more songbirds in cover crops planted for game[2-4]; twice as many butterflies and an increased number of flowering shrubs in woods managed for game[5,6]. Woodland management for pheasants also benefits some small mammals, such as wood mice and bank voles[7]. The provision of supplementary feed has positive effects on many seed-eating birds (see chapter 4), some of which are UK BAP priority species[8]. A GWCT study found that songbirds made a quarter of all animal visits to gamebird feeders[9].

What impact do these effects have?

As an example, the combined package of game management measures at the GWCT demonstration farm in Leicestershire increased the abundance and breeding density of several bird species, including blackbird, song thrush, dunnock, whitethroat, chaffinch and yellowhammer[10]. A further unpublished GWCT study looked at 34 farmland sites nearby, and found 30% more farmland birds on farms with shoots than on farms without[11].

Why are these positive effects seen?

Pheasants are birds of the woodland edge, and some evidence shows that new woodlands are more likely to be planted, and existing woodlands to be preserved and better managed in areas with pheasant shoots[1,12]. Generally, as well as game management providing food and reducing predation pressure, woodland management practices that provide suitable habitat for pheasants also improve habitat for these other species.

What are these management practices?

Pheasant management includes: reducing the canopy density (skylighting, thinning, coppicing) to allow more light into the wood, maintaining and widening woodland rides, more diversity at woodland edges, creating or maintaining hedgerows, planting game cover crops, controlling predators and providing supplementary food[1,12–16].
See chapter 4 for more detail.

What negative effects can pheasant releasing have on the local environment?

The area within and immediately surrounding a release pen often has a different profile of plants compared to areas with no pens. There is more bare ground, reduced low-level vegetation structure, and certain woodland plants are less common[13,17].

The vegetation within hedgerows can be affected by pheasants using them as corridors, particularly near to large release pens[18]. Other places where birds congregate are likely to see similar effects. Once released, pheasants (and red-legged partridges, see chapter 2) do eat insects[19] but do not necessarily affect insect populations. The range of beetle species found may be different in pheasant release pens compared to reference areas, with some species more numerous and some less[14].

These effects are seen for two reasons. The first is that lots of pheasants in one area scratch the ground, and their droppings add nutrients to the soil, acting as fertiliser in an area which would otherwise have quite nutrient-poor soil. This changes the makeup of the soil, which then supports different plants, so the presence of the pheasants can affect the environment, even if they are not directly eating the plants or insects. The second is that management of the woodland or other habitat for the pheasants can change the environment. Commonly game managers will open up the canopy in and around a woodland release pen and plant more shrubs to provide low cover. This may lead to fewer shade tolerant woodland plants, increased grassland plants and/or encourage a different ground invertebrate community.

The recommended stocking density for pheasant pens is no more than 1,000 birds per hectare. © GWCT

Although released pheasants will eat insects, they do not need them as they are usually given a balanced diet with plentiful feed. Most insects also hibernate during the winter so they are only available for a short period around September when the releases are still at their most abundant[20]. It is often suggested that woodland insects in general may still be negatively affected by large scale releases. In the most detailed study some small effects of releases on improved grassland alongside release woodlands were found, but there was very little impact on the woodland ground invertebrate community itself[19]. Another study found no obvious effect of large scale red-leg releases on nearby species rich grassland[21]. A 2015 study did find an impact on larger ground beetles inside release pens, with more grassland type beetles and fewer woodland ones. It is unclear what the mechanism for this was. Direct predation of beetles might be involved but it is perhaps more likely that a less shaded woodland floor and different ground vegetation in the pens was the main factor[14,17]. A few woodland butterflies feed (as caterpillars) on only one woodland plant species, for example violets. Avoid enclosing key colonies of these plants inside release pens.

Are there negative effects on other bird species?

It has been suggested that released pheasants may be involved in disease transmission to wild birds or that predation of other birds may be higher on pheasant shoots without good predator control. These are important questions for which there is currently little evidence. We await the scientific studies to investigate them.

What are the main recommendations for pheasant release?

Best practice states that pens should be stocked below a density of 1,000 poults per hectare (400 per acre). This is 10 square metres of space per bird, and is based on research examining the effects on woodland ground flora and husbandry considerations. Sites for release pens should be chosen to minimise damage, avoiding areas such as slopes and water courses, areas of conservation value or ecologically sensitive areas[16].

Where shoots exceed the recommended densities, they should be able to demonstrate that their particular circumstances and management regime (for example, limiting the period of time birds are in release pens) does not significantly damage woodland flora and fauna. Delaying the time of release can avoid some potential conflicts. For example, some reptile and butterfly colonies may be vulnerable in mid-to-late summer but less so if the gamebirds are released later. If in doubt take expert advice.

Release pens should occupy at most a third of the total woodland area on an estate. This means that most of the woodland benefits from the management but isn't damaged by the birds themselves. The 'total woodland area' used in this calculation could include scrub patches, substantial hedgerows with trees, shelter belts and new woodland plantings, but it should not include the central part of large woodland blocks where there is no game interest.

We recommend not moving release pens unless there are obvious conservation or welfare benefits to be gained. Birds released into woodland pens should be encouraged to leave the pen for at least part of the day once they are used to roosting in trees.

We recommend avoiding the release of more than 1,500 birds to funnel through one main hedgerow that links releasing and holding areas, particularly if that hedgerow contains a good ground flora and is home to valuable wildlife. For larger releases it is best to use several hedgerows or plant game cover crop 'lead-in' strips to widen linking habitats.

Shoots should generally avoid releasing birds into sensitive woodland habitat, in particular reptile breeding or hibernation sites, and patches that have unusual or important plant or insect species. In ancient semi-natural woodland we recommend no more than 700 birds per hectare in release pens.

Follow the Code

Releasing on SSSIs
"Shoot managers should be aware of SSSIs and other designated areas on their ground and should liaise with the landowner and the relevant statutory authorities to ensure they avoid potentially damaging activities"

Size of the bag
"Guns should take account of the size of bags and frequency of shooting."

How have stocking densities changed?
The GWCT published releasing guidelines following our concerns in 2005 that the average stocking density in release pens was 1,800 birds per ha, rather than the recommended 1,000[17]. It's our view that the trend in recent years has been towards lower stocking densities.

Overall, is pheasant release considered to be beneficial or detrimental to wildlife and the countryside?

On estates that operate good habitat management and release birds at sustainable densities, our evidence shows that there can be significant biodiversity benefits. There is certainly controversy around this, but a comprehensive RSPB review on this subject concludes: "the positive effects of habitat management are likely to result in a positive net conservation impact"[22].

How much woodland is managed for pheasants?

14% of the total UK woodland area is managed for pheasant shooting. This is 28% in England, and 4% in Scotland and Wales[23].

How many pheasants are released for shooting?

It is difficult to know precise numbers, but GWCT calculations estimate that around 43 million pheasants were released in 2012.

Do shoots which release greater numbers of birds and offer bigger bags do more harm than smaller ones?

This question has been increasingly debated as the popularity of driven shooting has grown and bag limits have been called for in some quarters. But this is to approach the problem of bad practice from the wrong angle. The key thing to remember is that where conservation value is concerned, it is not quantity but quality that matters. A big shoot releasing a large number of birds may have the freedom and resources to invest in impressive conservation measures, whereas a small shoot which is not observing release guidelines or doing associated conservation work, may be doing more harm than good. However, a big shoot has greater potential to be damaging to the environment, so in this sense has a greater responsibility to avoid that.

Equally, a shoot which releases more birds over a large area may be more beneficial than a shoot releasing fewer birds in a limited space. Similarly, bag size is not a proxy for conservation benefit. For example, it may cause less disturbance to shoot two large days in a season than 10 small days. The key is that in all cases shoots conform to best practice releasing densities, deliver conservation benefits, secure a market for the game and that respect for the quarry and consideration of the public is maintained at all times. In chapter 4 we look in more detail at the various conservation measures associated with shooting.

© Martin Clay

Pheasant numbers through the season

How many of the released pheasants are shot?

Estimates vary, but a recent GWCT analysis looking at 13 studies carried out over the past 20 years found that the return rate (number of pheasants released that are actually shot) was around 35%[25]. This will vary enormously between shoots, but the UK figures are good compared with release methods used elsewhere in the world. For example, one study in France found that UK-style open-topped release pens gave a return of shot birds about one third higher than the usual French method of using small, closed-topped pens for around a week[26].

What happens to the other birds?

The GWCT analysis also found that 19% of released pheasants were predated or scavenged before the shooting season began, mostly by foxes. Predation/scavenging continued throughout the winter, accounting for approximately another 15%. Fourteen percent died of other causes, for example accidents, disease and so on, and 16% survived the shooting season[25].

Figure 1: The fate of released pheasants

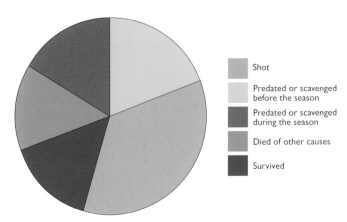

Shot

Predated or scavenged before the season

Predated or scavenged during the season

Died of other causes

Survived

Our analysis shows that 19% of released pheasants were predated or scavenged before the season, 35% shot, 15% predated or scavenged during the season, 14% died of other causes and 16% survived the season.

What happens to the surviving 16%?

Our analysis showed that almost half of the surviving hens were killed by predators between mid-March and mid-July. Ninety-five percent of these were killed by foxes. The proportion of surviving hens predated was heavily affected by the level of predator control performed – where predator control effort is low, 59% of surviving hens were predated, whereas where effort was high, 30% were predated[25].

One important point to bear in mind about this study is that the birds were followed by tagging to monitor their fate, with the tags attached to the birds at 10 weeks of age. This means that we do not know what had happened to any poults before that age. Raptor predation on gamebirds is thought to occur mainly between the ages of 7 and 10 weeks, so any effect is unlikely to have been captured in this study.

Does the number of birds on the ground decline throughout the season?

Yes. The graph on the facing page shows the loss of pheasants from release, through to the end of the season. There are five times fewer birds at the end of January than there were at the beginning of October when the shooting season began. Numbers fall as birds are shot throughout the season, as well as being lost to other causes. Therefore, Guns should expect to shoot smaller bags in January.

How many birds would have been released for each bird that is left at the end of January?

If shooting has occurred throughout the season, 16% of the released birds survive the season, so for each bird alive on the 31st of January, six were released the previous summer.

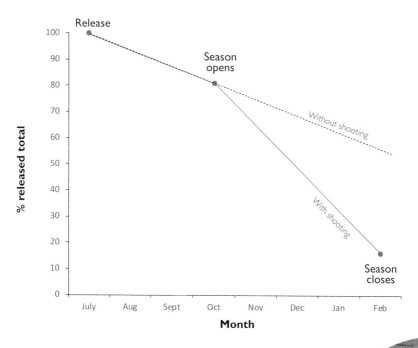

Figure 2: Number of pheasants throughout the season

© GWCT

Pheasant origins

Experts believe that the common pheasant was present in Britain as early as the 11th century, and that pheasants are likely to have been introduced by the Normans, rather than by the Romans as is often perceived. They have certainly been an important quarry species since the 16th century.

Did you know?

The expectation should be that bags will be smaller in January. © GWCT

Why big January days are a modern problem

- The current trend towards big days at the end of the season is not how it was in the past. Previously, Guns expected to shoot fewer birds in January, including cocks-only days to leave the hens and encourage remaining pheasants to breed. January birds were traditionally more challenging as they were stronger and wilier. It was a case of quality over quantity.
- In order to have enough birds to shoot large bags in January, many more need to be released at the beginning of the season, increasing the number lost to predation during the season, and meaning that many more birds will be left when shooting ceases.
- This inevitably makes it more difficult for the shoot to ensure it is complying with the animal welfare requirements to look after birds once the season has finished.

Wild pheasants

There are several ways of defining a wild pheasant: some are truly wild, hatched from parents that also hatched from wild birds. However, the offspring of birds which were reared and released and survived the shooting season may also be considered wild.

Partly because of this, it is difficult to calculate the number of truly wild pheasants in the UK. Indeed, rather than a clear division between released and wild birds, it could be seen as a continuum. Some estates specialise in producing wild pheasants and local populations exist in East Anglia, Kent, central-southern England, Lincolnshire, Yorkshire and north-eastern England.

Why should shoots support their wild bird population?
- Shoots have a duty of care for released birds after the end of the season. It is irresponsible to leave pheasants that you have released in a situation where they cannot find adequate food to survive. Failure to look after birds after the season finishes is currently one of the biggest ethical issues in shooting.
- Because management for wild birds helps improve biodiversity.
- It can reduce the number that need to be released.

How can surviving birds be supported?
Supplementary food should still be provided normally until the end of May to support any released birds left on the ground. Numbers of pheasants gradually drop throughout the spring until more are released the following summer. However, where supplementary food is provided alongside suitable breeding habitat and protection from nest predators through legal predation control, released birds can produce young of their own. More detail on these management techniques is given in chapters 3 and 4.

How many birds could a truly wild bird shoot hope to support?
Realistically, an effective wild bird management programme might result in 100-150 surviving chicks per square kilometre (km^2) of suitable wood or farmland habitat, in optimal circumstances.

What are the conservation benefits of wild pheasant management?

Habitat management, predator control and supplementary feeding in winter and spring have benefits for many other species and lead to increased biodiversity on wild bird shoots. The effect of management for wild pheasants at the Allerton Project in Leicestershire has been thoroughly studied, demonstrating that breeding songbirds were more abundant when game management was performed[10,27]. Some species that are in national decline responded dramatically to game management – for example the song thrush increased 243% in six years of management. Brown hare have also been monitored during periods of wild gamebird management, and in three separate experiments the hare populations have increased, responding particularly to predator control[28]. Also, areas managed for wild gamebirds do not receive some of the negative effects sometimes associated with releasing such as damage to woodland plants in release pens.

Follow the Code

Supplementary feeding

"Sufficient feed for released birds remaining after the end of the shooting season should be provided until adequate natural food is available normally to the end of May."

Is the UK's wild pheasant population growing, if it is added to each year by released birds?

It seems to be remaining stable, and the reasons behind this are a key area of ongoing research. Added to the effect of predation and other pressures which all wild birds face, breeding success in the UK released pheasant population is very low. Captive-bred birds who join the wild population do not breed well for various reasons[29,30]. Some evidence suggests that reared pheasants are more vulnerable to predation than wild ones[31], so predator control could be even more important. Captive bred birds are not usually as suited to survive and breed in the wild after the shooting season, physically or because of their behaviour. Current GWCT research aims to address this with updated rearing practices and shoot management.

Male pheasants hold territories in spring which attract a harem of females. © David Mason

Pheasant facts

Pheasants are between 53-89 cm in length, with males being the larger at over 66 cm. The tail is elongated in both sexes at 20-44 cm, but especially the male which is over 35 cm. Wing span is between 70 and 90 cm, again with the male being larger with wing span of more than 80 cm. Weight can vary, depending on local conditions, for example the provision of supplementary food, severity of winter etc. However, wild males usually weigh between 1-1.4 kg (Jan-Mar), and females around 0.9-1kg. Reared adult pheasants can weigh considerably more. The males have a loud, sharp disyllabic territorial crow call, which is similar but repeated as an alarm call[32].

In the wild, pheasants are omnivorous, eating grains, seeds, berries and other fruits, roots, green shoots, small arthropods, insects and molluscs. They mainly feed on the ground by scratching with their feet and digging with their beak. Chicks hatch with enough yolk present in their stomach to eat little for the first two days, although they will eat if they find food, after which they begin to eat insects and other invertebrates. Green plants and shoots are added to the diet after ten days, followed by grains and seeds after six weeks[32].

Male pheasants hold territories in spring which attract a harem of females. After mating, males are not involved in the breeding process. Hen pheasants lay clutches of 8-15 eggs from late March through to early June, nesting on the ground, usually in thick vegetation such as tall grass, scrub, hedge bottoms and arable crops. Incubation is for 23-25 days, from when the last egg is laid. Hatching is coordinated and all eggs hatch within around 12 hours of each other. The chicks are cared for by the female, but are self-feeding. They are able to fly from around 12 days, but remain with the female for at least two months[32].

Their flight is mostly adapted to giving them rapid escape when danger threatens. What they need for this is rapid acceleration, and good manoeuvrability to dodge trouble. The pheasant's long tail can act as a rudder, able to help steer it quickly through woodland. When threatened, pheasants can produce a sudden burst of power for around 8 seconds to lift them off the ground and out of danger, followed by a glide. The flight and glide will carry a pheasant about 400m over flat ground. After the exertion of this flight, the birds need about an hour to process the lactic acid that was produced in their flight muscles and recover, before they are able to fly properly again. For this reason, it is considered unsporting to drive them again too soon.

© Martin Clay

Chicks don't need to eat straight away
Pheasant or partridge eggs are usually laid one each day. Once the clutch is complete, the hen starts to incubate. The eggs that were laid first may have been in the nest for some time (up to 24 days in the case of red-legged partridge), but chick development begins when incubation starts, and the eggs all therefore hatch at a similar time.

When the chicks hatch, they do not need to eat for the first day or two because they have the remains of the egg yolk already in their stomach.

Ask the shoot

1. How many birds per hectare do you place in your release pens in the summer?

2. How much of the shoot's wooded area is fenced for release pens?

3. Do you have any SSSIs on the shoot?

4. How have you assessed the environmental impact of your release pens?

5. How far away is your poults supplier? Are they a member of the GFA?

6. How old are the birds I will be shooting, and when were they released?

7. Have any birds been replenished during the season on your shoot?

8. How many of last year's birds will I expect to see this season?

9. How often do you shoot the same drives?

10. Do you shoot fewer birds towards the end of the season?

11. How many shoot days do you have per week in January?

12. What is your average bag and what measures do you put in place to accommodate it?

13. How will you support the remaining birds at the end of this season?

14. What are you doing to support wild breeding pheasants?

Because they are released on farmland rather than in woodland, red-legs are perceived to have less potential for affecting their surroundings than pheasants. © *David Kjaer*

2. Red-legged partridges

The red-legged partridge (red-leg) was introduced to East Anglia in the late 18th Century, using stock from France. Although becoming well established by the end of the century, its spread across Britain was slow and its current distribution was not reached until the 1930s[33].

Released Red-legs

Can red-legs can be reared and released?

Yes. The species is a prolific breeder and is easily reared in captivity. In the wild, the hen can lay two clutches, one for incubation by herself and the other by the cock, so that each pair can produce two broods within a few weeks of each other[34]. This means that the red-leg is also a prolific egg-layer in captivity, making it attractive to rear and release. This became increasingly popular from the early 1960s as it was seen as a means of maintaining a partridge shoot despite the decline of the grey.

How many are released?

Red-legged partridges are reared and released across farmland in the

UK, and often form an important component of the bag. Estimates vary, but it is likely that somewhere in the region of 9 million red-legs are released each year[24].

How are they released?

Typically, birds are placed in pens in July or August at around 10-13 weeks of age where they are held for one to four weeks before release. Birds can all be released from a pen at the same time anywhere between 24 hours and three weeks after being placed in the pen. Alternatively, birds can be 'trickle' released whereby a small quantity of birds are released at a time while retaining a successively smaller number of birds in the pen.

The birds remaining in the pen call to the released birds, which helps prevent the released birds wandering off. Food is provided close to the pen to hold released birds in the vicinity. For red-legged partridges, there is a wide variety of approaches between shoots, with each having their own preferred strategy. Whatever technique is used, all releasing must be completed one month before the first shoot and pens removed.

In general red-legged partridges are usually released in smaller groups than pheasants, and from closed-top released pens. A medium to large shoot may use 20 or more pens containing 50 to 300+ birds per pen. Unlike pheasant releases, which take place in woodland, red-legs tend to be released over open country. This is usually arable farmland but can be grassland, with each pen associated with a specific block of dedicated game cover. On larger partridge shoots there may be several pens each containing several hundred birds feeding into one large block of cover.

Follow the Code

How old before shooting
"Red-legged partridges should be at least 15-16 weeks old before shooting to ensure fully mature, healthy and marketable game."

Siting pens
"Partridge release pens should be sited in cover crops on arable or improved grassland, rather than on semi-natural or unimproved habitats*."

*Note: 'unimproved habitat' refers to land which has typically not been ploughed, sown or had fertiliser spread on it. 'Improvement' is hard to reverse, and following this process, many important arable plants may be lost and are unlikely to return.

Why is this habitat difference important?

The impact of partridge releasing on the surrounding countryside has less well studied than that of pheasant releasing, partly because partridges are usually released onto open farmland. Farmland tends to be less biodiverse than woodland, so the release of red-legs here is perceived to have less potential for affecting the surroundings than pheasants, which may for instance be released into ancient semi-natural woodlands.

Is there evidence that red-leg release can have an effect on the environment?

Not many studies have been done, but one looked at the possible impact of red-leg release on the number of Adonis blue butterflies on chalk grassland. The Adonis blue is scarce and declining, and has been made a "priority species" under the UK Biodiversity Action Plan[36]. They are found on warm, south-facing slopes of chalk grassland in the UK. Gamebird release pens are sometimes sited close to these areas, with the birds then roaming nearby, so the Adonis blue has been highlighted as a species potentially at risk from gamebird release[21].

To look into this, GWCT scientists carried out a three-year study examining the differences between areas where large numbers of red-legs were released and ones where no or very few were released. It found that the vegetation was shorter in areas with gamebirds present[21]. The released partridges did eat general insects on the chalk grassland, but the study did not find an overall effect of this on the insect populations. The authors suggested that the impact on butterflies may be higher than they were able to show, put forward reasons for not detecting an effect, and proposed further studies.

What are the main recommendations when releasing red-legs?

Avoid placing release pens or partridge feeders within 500m of areas of high conservation value such as ancient hedgerows, chalk grassland, lowland heath or other sensitive habitats. Allow a buffer zone of game crop or other cover to keep concentrations of birds away from the hedge. Partridge pens should be removed before shooting begins so they cannot be used for topping up, to prevent a mistaken assumption that they are being used for that purpose, and as they tend to be unsightly.

Wild red-legged partridges

How many wild red-legs are there in the UK?

The current status of the wild red-legged partridge in Britain is difficult to assess because of the scale of releasing. The continuum between released and wild birds discussed above with respect to pheasants also applies. Nevertheless, there seems to have been a decline, at least since 1985. The most recent estimates of population size in Britain are approximately 82,000 pairs[37].

Why is population size important for an introduced species?

Despite its introduced status, conservation of the red-legged partridge in Britain is important because the natural range of the species is restricted almost entirely to Spain, Portugal and France, where numbers are declining[38]. Although the red-leg may be a more prolific breeder than the grey, when breeding in the wild their nests are not well concealed, and they may therefore be exposed to higher rates of predation[39].

Where do wild red-legs live in Britain?

As one would expect from its Mediterranean origin, the red-legged partridge thrives on dry, sandy soils and breeds best in areas of high summer temperatures (where the average daily high temperature in July exceeds 19°C), being generally the Eastern part of the British lowlands.

What nesting habitat do they use?

Red-legs prefer to nest in hedgerows with nettles and good cover; and taller vegetation that gives more protection from crow predation[40]. Overhead vegetation is very important, especially if thorny. When preferred nest sites are not available, red-legs will nest in crops, which can lead to lower nest success[39].

Did red-leg partridge experience the same historical declines as greys?

We do not have reliable data to show exactly what has happened to the national population over the years. In the 1950s and 60s, wild grey partridge suffered population declines for several reasons (see chapter 3). It is likely that wild red-legs suffered like greys from the removal of hedgerows and enlargement of fields because this would have reduced their nesting habitat. On the other hand, red-legs are perhaps less vulnerable to the loss of chick-food insects from farmland than grey partridges, because their chicks' diet consists more of grass and seeds rather than being dependent on insects as grey partridge chicks are[41].

Can red-leg shooting impact grey partridge conservation?

One area of concern around released red-leg shooting is the accidental shooting of wild grey partridges. This concern is not new: for many years the GWCT has warned its members of the dangers of overshooting wild grey partridges when releasing red-legs[42]. One study found that intensive shooting of red-legs led to grey partridge autumn losses of 35–39%[43]. This would have serious effects for local grey partridge stocks, however the same study also showed that improving education and awareness could reduce grey partridge losses to well below 20%[43].

As part of the GWCT's grey partridge restoration project at Royston from 2002-2010, the impact of shooting red-legs on the restored grey partridge stock was studied. The whole demonstration area was intensively managed for grey partridge, including the provision of nesting, foraging and winter cover, supplementary feeding and predator control. Shoot days were targeted at red-legs and pheasants, and measures were taken to avoid inadvertent shooting of grey partridge. This showed that, when carried out carefully, over 60% of red-legs could be shot while keeping grey partridge losses under 5%. From 2004 to 2008, grey partridge loss rates averaged 2.7%[44].

On this site, the pair density of grey partridges quadrupled with partridge management. The income from red-leg shooting was able to offset some of the costs of this, whilst not preventing grey partridge recovery. The key to avoiding grey partridge losses with red-leg shooting is in the Guns' ability to tell the species apart when they fly, or to show restraint if they are not sure that the bird they are shooting is a red-leg. At Royston, the shoots were arranged to avoid driving greys wherever possible, and if the beaters identified that grey partridges were in the drive, a whistle was used to alert the Guns.

How do I tell red-legs and greys apart on the shoot?

Red-legs scatter when flushed, and are slower, lower flying birds than the grey, tending to fly singly over Guns. Educating the Guns in this regard is very important, along with warning them if drives are mixed.

Red-leg facts

Slightly bigger than its grey counterpart, the red-legged partridge is 32-34 cm in length, with a wingspan of 47-50 cm; the male is larger than the female. Distinguishing the red-leg from the grey partridge is easy in good light and on open ground, but can be more difficult when the bird is in flight as the tail pattern is identical[32].

The red-leg prefers low or open vegetation, but is adaptable and lives on a wide variety of open landscapes across its natural range. In the UK, open farmland is its usual habitat including arable fields and pasture. The red-leg is resident all year round[32].

Red-legs feed mainly on grain, seeds, leaves and roots, with insects being of lesser importance to chicks than they are to grey partridge chicks. In the first two weeks after hatching, insects make up approximately 30% of the red-leg chick diet.

Breeding red-legs are usually monogamous and form long-term pair bonds. Pairs are formed in February or March, and eggs are laid in late April or May. Their nests are a shallow scrape lined with small amounts of vegetation, often built by the male. Eggs are laid roughly 1.5 days apart. Clutch size ranges from 10 to 16 eggs, with an average of 11 eggs per clutch in England. Incubation begins when the clutch is complete, and lasts 23-24 days. Red-legs can lay two clutches, one incubated by the male and one by the female – this is thought to happen in 20-40% of pairs in southern England. If one clutch is laid, incubation is by the female[32].

The young are mobile from hatching and the family group move off the nest soon after all chicks have hatched. Chicks largely self-feed, and are brooded when small by either parent. They are capable of flight at around 10 days, reach full adult size in around 2 months, and remain with their parents throughout the winter[32].

© David Kjaer

Ask the shoot

1. How old are your red-legs when you commence shooting?

2. Are your partridge pens sited next to sensitive areas or hedgerows?

3. Do you release partridges after the season has started?

4. Do you feed until the end of May to support your red-legs after the season?

5. What do you do to encourage your wild red-leg population?

6. Do you have wild greys on your shoot? If so what are you doing to prevent them being shot accidentally?

7. Are all partridge release pens taken down before shooting starts?

Grey partridges are an "indicator species" for broader farmland biodiversity, because where they thrive, a range of other species tend to do well. © Markus Jenny

3. Grey partridge

In the past, the wild grey partridge thrived on farmland, and was traditionally the main focus of shooting in the lowlands. Management for driven partridge shooting led to rising numbers during the 19th century; it involved comprehensive predator control in a farmed environment that provided good partridge habitat, with weedy cereal crops, traditional crop rotations including grass crops, small fields separated by hedges, fallows and waste ground. By contrast, grey partridge numbers have been falling in the UK throughout the second half of the 20th century, with the decline becoming most marked since the mid-1960s. To focus conservation efforts, the grey partridge was put on the UK Red Data List in 1990, became a priority species under the 1995 UK Biodiversity Action Plan[36], and remains a red-listed Bird of Conservation Concern. Progress has been made in areas that make a commitment to partridge conservation, but overall the decline in their numbers continues.

GWCT research on grey partridge declines in the 1960s and 1970s helped to establish the new field of agro-ecology, which is studying ecology within farming systems. Scientific study moved from recording declines, to investigating the changes in the arable environment that were affecting partridges[45-47]. This work found that the causes of the grey partridge decline were directly or indirectly related to much wider declines in many aspects of farmland biodiversity. For instance, the UK government monitors national bird abundance through the British Trust for Ornithology's Breeding Bird Survey, which has shown a 92% decline in numbers of grey partridge from 1967 to 2015, in conjunction with declines in many other species of farmland bird[48].

Several conservation measures developed with partridges in mind have been incorporated into agri-environment schemes. © Peter Thompson

Why is the wild grey partridge so important?

Although the grey partridge now makes up a much smaller component of the bag than it used to, and relatively few people may ever go to a grey partridge shoot, it is a very important species in both the history of shooting, and the evolution of game management techniques. It is our native gamebird, and forms part of shooting's heritage. The grey partridge population is declining, and focused conservation efforts are needed if we are to recover the population, but there is also a wider relevance for grey partridge conservation.

Grey partridges are an "indicator species" for broader farmland biodiversity, because where they thrive, other species tend to do well, and where they are declining, other species also tend to struggle. Partridge declines are mirrored by declining numbers of many other farmland bird species, and introducing partridge conservation measures often leads to wider biodiversity benefits. For example, areas which are managed with partridge-friendly techniques such as conservation headlands can also have higher numbers of songbirds[39,49], butterflies[50,51] and rare arable plants[52,53]. Because of this, the partridge has been labelled the "Barometer of the Countryside"[39].

Furthermore, because of GWCT research into grey partridge declines and how we might help this species, several conservation measures developed with grey partridge in mind, such as beetle banks and conservation headlands, have been incorporated into agri-environment schemes in the UK. The fact that financial support is available for these conservation techniques means that they are likely to be more widespread across the countryside, benefiting more gamebirds and wildlife.

How have grey partridge numbers changed?

In the last two hundred years the grey partridge population in the UK shows four distinct trends in different periods. These reflect changes in management of predators and of the wider countryside: early 1800s to late 1800s, an increase in numbers; late 1800s to pre-1950s, generally high numbers; 1950-1970, sharp decline in numbers; and after 1970, a continued gradual decline[39,54,55].

Why has this decline happened?

The 1950s saw the widespread introduction of herbicides in arable farming, which eliminated arable weeds from crops and reduced the abundance of invertebrates that live on those weeds. As grey partridge chicks depend on invertebrates for their survival during the first two weeks of life, and as in arable areas the chicks forage primarily in cereal crops, this was a major disruption to the grey partridge food chain (see Figure 3 overleaf)[56].

Grey partridge chick survival, which averaged 49% before the introduction of herbicides, dropped to 32% on average once their use became widespread[54]. In the 1980s, the use of summer insecticide treatments on cereal crops also became more frequent, which reduced the abundance of chick-food invertebrates in those crops even further[57,58]. Also from the 1950s onwards, the increasing mechanisation of agriculture led to the removal of hedgerows and other field boundaries to make fields bigger and farming more efficient, which meant a loss of nesting cover for grey partridges[45,46].

Figure 3: The grey partridge food chain

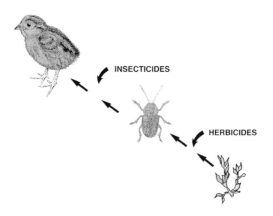

INSECTICIDES

HERBICIDES

The third cause of the decline is increased predation pressure from generalist predators such as fox, stoat, weasel, rat, magpie and carrion/hooded crow. As chick survival dropped with agricultural changes, autumn grey partridge stocks also dropped, so shoot management increasingly turned away from wild birds in favour of released pheasants and red-legged partridges in order to sustain bags. Reducing the number of partridge predators, which was part of the traditional role of the gamekeeper, stopped or became less intensive. See chapter 5 for more information on predation control. This led to an increase in predation pressure[59], particularly on incubating females and their eggs, which was exacerbated by the lower availability of nesting habitat[45,46].

Hence there were three causes of the decline of the grey partridge in the UK, and these were described as the "three-legged stool": a fall in chick-food invertebrates, a reduction in nesting cover, and a rise in predation pressure. For partridge conservation, all three of these issues must be addressed – a three legged stool will only stand with all three legs in place.

Why is it continuing?

These changes to farming methods mean that the resources partridges depend on are now scarce on most modern farmland. The loss of hedgerows and field edges has led to large open fields with little nesting cover. Modern spraying regimes for arable crops leave few arable weeds and few invertebrates within a much more uniform farmed landscape, where it is harder for partridge chicks to find food in the summer, and adults to find food or cover in the winter. The abundance of generalist predators is higher now than it was 50 years ago[48,60], see chapter 5.

Why are grey partridges on the quarry list when they are in national decline?

Shooting can be a powerful incentive to conserve and reverse local declines of a species. The areas with the most grey partridges in the UK are those where the most grey partridges are shot. This is because shooting motivates land managers to perform active conservation for them, in the form of habitat management (provision of nesting cover, insect-rich brood-rearing habitat, winter food and cover) and predation control[55]. The Code of Good Shooting Practice calls for a moratorium on shooting wild grey partridges where they are not being conserved and when the local population is below 20 birds per 100 ha in autumn.

Figure 4: Grey Partridge index from NGC bags
(1826-2008)

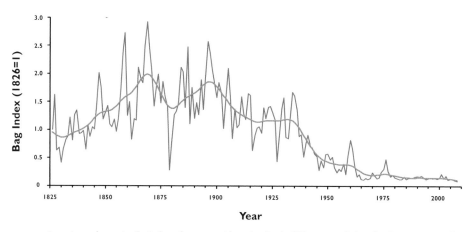

Long-term change in the index of grey partridges shot in the UK, as recorded in the GWCT National Gamebag Census. Numbers were high from around 1880 to World War 2, because farming methods and intense gamekeeping produced an environment in which grey partridges could thrive. Even if gamekeeping activity were comparable, a conventionally farmed modern landscape cannot support the same numbers as in the past.

Can we release grey partridge to boost the wild population?

Generally, no, because the survival of reared and released grey partridges is poor in the wild, as is the breeding success of any survivors[67,68]. Grey partridge release could even be counter-productive for the local wild population, so shoots should take expert advice.

The first recommendation in the GWCT guidelines for re-establishing grey partridge through releasing is *"Where grey partridges are still present (over two pairs/km² on at least 4 km²), releasing is inappropriate."* Under these circumstances, partridge recovery can and should be brought about by habitat improvements and predator management. For example, a GWCT demonstration project at Royston (2002-2010) increased the local grey partridge spring population density from 2.9 to over 18 pairs per km² in five years[44].

> ## Follow the Code
> ### Stop shooting
> *"Wild grey partridges should only be shot where they are actively conserved, and autumn stocks are above 20 birds per 100 hectares. Shooting should stop to prevent populations falling below this threshold."*

What can be done to support wild grey partridges?

Many years of scientific research, experiments and demonstration sites have shown what is needed to support wild grey partridge conservation within a modern farming environment. Suitable partridge habitat should provide adequate cover for nesting, brood foraging and shelter from adverse weather and predators. All of these habitats are increasingly rare on farmland, for example with the loss of hedgerows, weeds from crops and overwinter stubbles.

Partridge-friendly management needs to address all three legs of the three-legged stool, otherwise it will collapse! Hence taking each one in turn:

What nesting habitat do they need?

Partridge breeding density is closely associated with the amount of nesting cover available[61]. The best nesting location is in thick tussocky grass cover, often at the base of a field boundary or on low banks slightly raised above the general field level. The site needs to be dry, sheltered and well concealed, with plenty of "residual" grass – dead grass from the previous year that helps with camouflage[39]. Beetle banks, hedgerows with rank vegetation at their base or perennial grassy cover at the edge of fields are all suitable. See chapter 4 for further information.

The loss of nesting cover in the modern countryside is one of the driving forces behind partridge declines. For the grey partridge population to recover to the target set by the 1995 Biodiversity Action Plan, computer models show that there would need to be 6.9 kilometres of nesting cover per km², along with 5% of arable land being insect-rich brood rearing cover[47,62]. The average amount of hedgerow on typical arable farmland is 4 kilometres per km² so there would need to be a substantial increase, or addition of other nesting cover[46,62].

What brood-rearing habitat do they need?

Grey partridge chicks need to eat lots of insects during the first two weeks of life for strong growth and high survival. They need insect-rich habitats near their nesting areas, where the hen can lead her chicks when they hatch to forage for food and seek shelter. Brood-rearing cover can be provided by conservation headlands, game crops such as strips or blocks of wild bird mix, or other forms of open, insect-rich vegetation that give both food and shelter at the same time. The structure of the vegetation in these foraging habitats is very important – it must have an upper canopy for protection, with an open structure underneath to allow chicks easy passage[52,63].

How can predation be reduced?

Being ground-nesting, breeding partridges are very vulnerable to predation. In conjunction with the provision of nesting cover, carrying out legal predator control to reduce numbers of generalist predators during the breeding season can ease this pressure and ensure that the grey partridge can fulfil its naturally high breeding potential[64].

Is there anything else?

At the same time, the provision of overwinter cover in the form of game cover crops, wild bird seed mixes, green manure or winter fodder crops provides food and protection from the weather and predators in winter months. The risk of predation by raptors is highest in February and March, when many sources of cover are ploughed up as part of normal farm practice. Good cover needs to be sufficiently high (approx. 30 cm), stand throughout the winter rather than die down, and ideally provide a steady accessible supply of nutritious seeds all winter. Supplementary food in hoppers also helps birds bridge the "hungry gap" at the end of the winter, in February/March[65,66].

How do shoots know if their partridges are responding?

The key to understanding how well partridges are responding is to monitor their numbers and breeding success. Typically, this is done by counting them in spring and again in autumn. We encourage anyone interested in partridge management to join our Partridge Count Scheme (PCS). This has been running for 85 years, and coordinates partridge counts across the UK. Members of the PCS receive advice on how to count and manage grey partridges. Based on their annual count data, PCS members receive feedback on management, and information on regional and national trends against which to compare their own results[55,69]. They also contribute towards a better understanding of the current status of grey partridges on farms across the country. For more information about the PCS, see chapter 8.

How is the grey partridge doing nationally?

Nationally, the species continues to decline because too few land managers have put in place partridge-friendly management. However, the numbers recorded by PCS members show how effective partridge management measures can be. Between 2000 and 2010, the UK grey partridge population declined by 40% - down by nearly a half. Over the same period, partridge numbers on PCS sites increased by 81%[55].

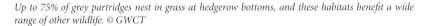

Up to 75% of grey partridges nest in grass at hedgerow bottoms, and these habitats benefit a wide range of other wildlife. © GWCT

Why is there such a difference?

Members of the PCS have a particular interest in partridge conservation. They receive advice and guidance about how to support their partridges, and incorporate these techniques into their farming methods. On PCS farms, there are more management and habitat features such as grassy margins, beetle banks, brood-rearing cover, wild bird cover, winter cover, predator control and supplementary feeding[70]. The resulting difference in partridge numbers between PCS and non-PCS sites shows that these measures can be effective[55].

In a study, soon to be published, we classified PCS sites into those with a shooting interest (partridges shot in at least half the years – 753 sites) and those without (no birds reported shot – 547 sites). We calculated an index of grey partridge pairs to represent their numbers between 2000 and 2015, which rose by 91% on shoots, but dropped by 18% on sites with no shooting. In comparison, the BTO index of grey partridge numbers declined by 54% over the same time period. This means that the number of partridge nearly doubled on PCS sites that shoot, dropped slightly on PCS sites that don't shoot, and dropped by half across the country.

Are current PCS sites enough to reverse the UK population decline?

Sadly not. Although partridge conservation efforts have led to local gains on PCS sites, they are too few to influence the national downward trend. To slow or reverse the national decline, we need much more widespread application of conservation measures to support grey partridges[62]. These would also benefit many other declining farmland wildlife species[39,49].

© *Jen Brewin*

Between 2000 and 2010, UK grey partridge population declined by 40%. Over the same period Partridge Count Sites achieved an 81% increase in partridge numbers and farmland bird species on PCS sites was 24% higher.

On the GWCT demonstration site at Rotherfield, farmland songbirds of conservation concern increased by 66% over six years.

Does the grey partridge management package benefit other species too?

Yes. Management that is designed or performed with one particular species in mind often has wide-ranging benefits for others sharing the same environment. The grey partridge is considered to be an indicator species for the farmland ecosystem. Where partridges do well, biodiversity tends to be higher than where partridges are struggling.

Conservation measures designed for partridges also provide support for other farmland wildlife. For example, improved nesting habitat for partridges along hedgerows or beetle banks also provides nest sites for harvest mice[71]. Wild bird seed mixes and food hoppers designed to provide winter food for partridges also help other seed-eating farmland birds during the winter and through the "hungry gap"[4,72]. One study found that the number of farmland bird species on PCS sites was 24% higher, with a greater variety of species, than on matched reference sites[49].

At the GWCT's Rotherfield grey partridge restoration project (2010-present), farmland bird surveys were conducted to examine the effect of gamebird management on avian biodiversity. These showed that farmland songbirds of conservation concern (such as yellowhammer, skylark, linnet and house sparrow) increased by 66% across the study area over six years[73]. Partridge management is also beneficial for rare arable plants. On modern arable land, many previously common flowering plants are now seldom seen, but rare species can reappear in conservation headlands and uncultivated field margins, for example: cornflower, night-flowering catchfly, narrow-fruited cornsalad and prickly poppy[52,53].

Did you know?

The fossil record indicates that grey partridges evolved on the steppes of Eurasia at least 2 million years ago and spread westward, with grey partridge remains dated to 475,000 years ago identified at Boxgrove in Sussex by John Stewart[39]. Evidence points to them being continuously present in Britain since the last ice age (summarised in Potts 2012).

The combined measures: a successful package

When implemented as a package, the management measures designed to satisfy the needs of grey partridges throughout the year can be very successful in increasing local partridge abundance. Several GWCT projects have implemented the management package to restore grey partridge numbers, including the Royston grey partridge recovery project, the Rotherfield partridge restoration project and the Peppering partridge project in West Sussex. All three studies have successfully produced at least a six-fold increase in grey partridge breeding pairs on their managed land after five to ten years of management.

These successes are not confined to GWCT "demonstration" projects, as impressive results are also achieved by farms that have implemented the three aspects of the management package. Across the Partridge Count Scheme (PCS), trends in local partridge abundance contrast with the national decline[55]. One particular example is an estate in Eastern England where the partridge management package was implemented in 2001, when partridge counts were 4.7 pairs per km². After ten years of management, this had risen to 54 pairs per km² in 2011. Spring stocks continue to increase at this site, despite the commencement of shooting at a sustainable level[74].

Another example of private partridge management is shown in the graph overleaf. Five estates in Norfolk began partridge management in 1992 (blue line), with five unmanaged estates in the same area for comparison (red line). In 1997, two of these control estates also began partridge management and saw their densities rise (green line)[62].

On the Peppering Partridge Project (pictured below) in West Sussex, grey partridge numbers increased from 13 birds across 1000 ha in 2003 to 1,852 in 2010 © GWCT

Perhaps the best known recent example is that of the Peppering partridge project on the GWCT's Sussex Study[39,75]. Here, implementation of habitat and management to benefit grey partridges has resulted in the restoration of a wild grey partridge shoot in southern England. Numbers of grey partridges in the autumn have increased from a low of 13 birds across 1000 ha in 2003 to 1852 grey partridges in 2010[75], with a sustainable shootable surplus since then.

Figure 5: Grey Partridge spring density

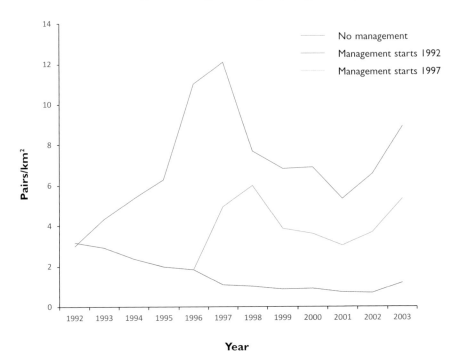

Average annual spring density (pairs/km²) of grey partridges on five estates in Norfolk where partridge management began in 1992 (blue line), and on five unmanaged estates from the same area (red line), 1992-2003. In 1996, two of the formerly unmanaged estates started management (green line).

Supplementary food in hoppers helps the birds in winter and during the "hungry gap" from February to the end of May
© Chris Knights

Grey partridge facts

The grey partridge is a medium-sized gamebird, being 29-31 cm in length with a 45-48 cm wingspan. The grey and brown plumage camouflages the bird well and it can be difficult to spot at a distance. The typical call is a harsh and repeated metallic sound referred to as a "Skirl-call", but grey partridges also have a range of other sounds, which include alarm calls, feeding calls or calls for gathering chicks[32].

The grey partridge lives in areas of low open vegetation interspersed with taller and denser patches such as cereals, hedgerows, scrub or rushes for cover. Grey partridges in the open are usually found within close proximity of taller or denser 'escape' cover. In the UK, grey partridges are resident throughout the year. They form pairs in early spring and stay together as a family group (covey), with their young and sometimes other lone adults throughout the summer and following winter. In January or February, the coveys break up and some dispersal occurs before territories are established and new pairs formed. The grey partridge is one of only two UK breeding bird species to stay in family groups over winter[32].

Egg-laying begins at the end of April or early May in a nest made by the female and formed by a shallow depression lined with grass and leaves in thick vegetation, such as is found at the base of a hedgerow or on a tussocky beetle bank[32].

The grey partridge lays the largest clutch of breeding birds in Britain, with 10-20 eggs, and an average clutch size of 15. If the eggs of the first clutch are lost, the female may lay a second, which will be smaller. Eggs are laid at 1-2 day intervals, and covered with nest material while laying continues. Incubation starts soon after the last egg is laid and lasts 23-25 days. Eggs are incubated by the female, while her mate remains on guard nearby. Once the young hatch they are cared for by both parents, and brooded when small. The chicks are mobile as soon as they hatch and leave the nest within a few hours, feeding themselves as they follow their parents. They become capable of fluttering off the ground at approximately 10 days, and of strong flight after 15 days[32].

Adult grey partridges feed predominantly on plant materials – green leaves of grasses, cereals and clover, and grain and weed seeds – with occasional insects. Most feeding occurs around dawn and dusk. Chick diet in the first two weeks is markedly different, containing a high proportion of insects in the diet. It is this early reliance on insects that is key to understanding the importance of chick-food resources in grey partridge conservation[46,76].

Adult flight is swift and strong, but usually short, up to a maximum of 1.5-2 kilometres. Even this distance is rarely seen, and usually only when birds are trying to escape from a predator (or shoot drive)[32], possibly in conjunction with particular weather conditions such as low temperatures. Grey partridges usually walk or run on the ground, interspersed with short linking flights a few metres above the ground. They roost communally – either in pairs, coveys or groups, tending to move to different sites each night – often in the middle of fields[77].

Ask the shoot

1. Do you have wild grey partridges on your shoot, if yes how many per 100 ha according to autumn counts?

2. If not, have you considered reintroduction?

3. If you do have wild grey partridges, what are you doing to support them what management plan do you have?

4. Are you releasing grey partridges?

5. Are you shooting your wild grey partridges? If so, do you comply with GWCT guidelines on sufficient numbers?

6. Which drives might there be wild greys on?

7. Are you a member of the Partridge Count Scheme?

Conservation headlands at the field edge (above and left) are sprayed with fewer pesticides, and so contain wildflowers and other plants, which support insects that in turn provide food for wild bird chicks © Jen Brewin

4. Habitat management

Managing game successfully means providing for the needs of the birds year-round, and to achieve this, the three-legged stool described earlier that was first identified for wild grey partridge (see page 42) has been applied in a broader fashion to game management. All gamebirds need:

1. Suitable habitat;
2. Enough food;
3. Tolerable levels of predation.

Shoot management that includes all three of these elements will not only support gamebirds, but have benefits for other wildlife. The standard shoot management approach of planting game cover crops, providing supplementary feed and performing predator control addresses these needs. Improvements benefiting gamebirds but also for other wildlife can always be made, and slight adjustments to the details of management (for example, what species to choose to provide foraging cover) can make all the difference. The Code of Good Shooting Practice recommends that shoot managers should prepare an appropriate, whole shoot management plan to ensure positive environmental benefits from their activities.

The gamekeeper's role

As well as organising shoot days and managing their gamebirds, from when they arrive on the shoot to when they go to the game dealer, the gamekeeper should be a working conservationist. Much of his or her time outside of shoot days is spent on activities which benefit not just the pheasants and partridges but a host of other wildlife. This fact is central to how the gamekeeping community sees itself, evidenced by the National Gamekeepers' Organisation motto "Keeping the Balance", which refers to enhancing biodiversity in the countryside. The guiding principle of "working conservation" is that wildlife can thrive alongside other land uses. The GWCT recognised that gamekeepers were the unexpected champions of this multiple outcomes approach as farming modernised to meet the post-war demand for food. It carefully studied how they began to use their range of techniques, to maintain their bird numbers without hindering farm production. Today these gamekeeping techniques are vital conservation tools because they support wildlife in a working countryside.

The cost of employing a gamekeeper is taken on by the shoot. Therefore, the conservation benefits that come from their work contribute to the public good at no additional cost to the taxpayer. This chapter looks in detail at the wide range of conservation activities undertaken by keepers to better understand what goes on outside shoot days and the key role it plays in wildlife management.

The farmer's role

The gamekeeper can only achieve a good habitat for his gamebirds and surrounding wildlife by working closely with the landowner, farmer and shoot manager. A range of jobs from drilling and maintaining game cover crops, to hedge maintenance and tree planting are often done by farm employees or contractors, so it is essential that the work schedule and any planting plans are agreed between the gamekeeping and farming operations. In many cases they will also make joint decisions on applications for agri-environment funding. In addition, the farm's commercial operations can impact game and wildlife on the shoot, from crop rotations to spraying regimes. Therefore, for both shooting and conservation to work, co-operation between everyone involved is essential and the most successful wildlife restoration projects always have a good working relationship between the farmer and keeper at their heart.

A good relationship with the farmer is essential to achieve a good habitat for gamebirds and other farmland wildlife. © GWCT

Suitable habitat – the right environment

Good habitat management is critical to gamebirds, and can also have a profound effect on the environment, with benefits for other wildlife. Planting and managing vegetation in such a way that it gives a suitable physical environment, or one that nurtures other resources such as a rich source of chick-food insects provides the habitat that gamebirds and other wildlife need to thrive.

Gamebirds need three types of habitat: foraging habitat, winter cover and, for wild birds, nesting cover. Some crops can provide for more than one of these needs at the same time.

What is a cover crop?

The term "cover crops" can be confusing, as it has two meanings – in farming, a cover crop is planted in winter to protect the soil from erosion, and improve nutrient retention, soil health and structure. In game management, it is an unharvested area planted for the benefit of game birds, providing food or shelter. For clarity, we use the term game cover crop in this book.

Typically planted in strips along the edge of fields or in blocks, for example between nesting habitat and farm crops, game cover crops provide food for the birds and protection from predators. Some also stand through the winter and give shelter from poor weather. Whichever game cover crop is chosen needs to have a suitable structure which can provide shelter from above but also allow ease of movement and foraging at ground level.

Farms with a significant pheasant interest typically plant 2-6% of their farmland with game cover crops. In some areas without pheasant releasing, crop diversity and the food and shelter available on farmland can be very limited. On estates managing for wild grey partridge, it is recommended that at least 7% of their land is under habitat management – this includes nesting cover, foraging cover and winter cover.

© GWCT

Game cover crops provide food and shelter from predators during the winter months.
© *Peter Thompson*

Game cover crops

Many species are available to use as game cover crops, and different ones offer different benefits and drawbacks. The best approach is usually a mix of several species, and we recommend that a shoot has a range of species, to provide a broad range of habitats for the gamebirds but also to benefit a wider range of other wildlife. This is a brief summary of the main points about some of the commonly used crops.

Maize
A reliable crop for holding game, which allows good control of broad-leaved weeds, so can be useful in a cover crop rotation. However, maize has several disadvantages. It can attract rats and badgers and dies down by Christmas so does not provide cover later in the winter. It also has very limited benefits for birds and other wildlife, so is not funded in agri-environment schemes.

Sorghum/dwarf grain sorghum
Sorghum can also be kept clear of broad-leaved weeds, and does not have cobs so is unattractive to rats. Some varieties of dwarf sorghum produce seed heads and they stand well throughout the winter. However, most varieties have no feed value, so hopper feeding will also be required. Sorghums do not like cold, wet summers.

Millet
Millet is a fantastic addition to any cover crop mix as gamebirds and small birds love the seed. Red millet ripens and sheds seed first, so is good for partridge cover. White millet seed lasts in the head much longer and can still be available to eat in January. A mix can provide seeds through the winter. Millet does not like heavy, wet soils.

Kale
Grown well, kale is the king of game cover crops – especially if it is left into a second year. It provides warm cover, is very hardy and produces stacks of small seeds that many birds love to eat. Great to include in a mix, and is economic as it lasts for two years. But it can be difficult to establish.

© GWCT

Triticale

Triticale is a hybrid wheat/rye crop which stands right through the winter – only heavy snow knocks it over, so it offers a good food supply well into the new year for a wide range of birds. It grows well on poor ground, does not need much nutrient to thrive and is excellent to use as part of a mix. Rabbits, hares and deer don't like to eat it when it is growing. But it can attract rats, rooks and pigeons.

Quinoa

Quinoa is easy to grow and ideal to plant as part of a mix, as it provides a good amount of nutritious seed. However, it does not offer much cover and little remains of the crop by January.

Sunflowers

Offers a wonderful sight through until the autumn and produces stacks of seed, which game and small birds love to eat. Consider the dwarf, multi-headed varieties. It does not offer much cover, so should be included as part of a mix with other crops that provide warmth.

Fodder radish

A fast-growing crop, which is ideal to include within a mix. The pods are slow to ripen, so seeds are not eaten until late in the year when many other seeds have gone. The seed is loved by many bird species. However, it can become too much of a good thing if too high a seed rate is used, dominating other species in the mix.

Take advice in designing a range of cover crops to provide for the needs of the birds year-round. This is available from the GWCT Advisory Department.

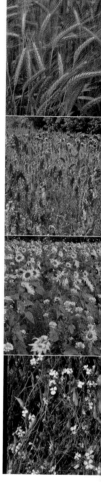

© GWCT

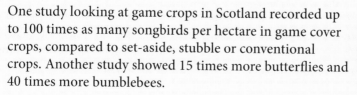

One study looking at game crops in Scotland recorded up to 100 times as many songbirds per hectare in game cover crops, compared to set-aside, stubble or conventional crops. Another study showed 15 times more butterflies and 40 times more bumblebees.

Conservation headlands may be drilled more widely to enable game bird chicks to move freely through them. © Peter Thompson/GWCT

Foraging habitat: for food

Foraging areas should provide a good food supply, either for adult birds or chicks, with sufficient cover for the foraging birds to be safe. Adult and young gamebirds have different dietary needs, with adults eating mainly seeds and plants, and chicks eating mostly insects and other invertebrates.

This dietary difference is particularly pronounced for grey partridge[78]. It is important to make sure there is plenty of suitable foraging area to provide chick-food insects in spring, and sufficient seeds and grains for adults year-round.

What sort of foraging cover?

Increasing the food supply for both adult birds in the winter, and chicks in the spring and summer, can be done by providing the right sort of foraging cover. Hens need brood-rearing cover that is rich in chick-food insects to lead their chicks to in the first days and weeks of their lives. Adults need areas that provide a sufficient supply of grains and seeds throughout the winter. These can be provided by conservation headlands and game cover crops.

How is this provided?

There are different techniques to provide these areas, mainly consisting of conservation headlands and game cover crops.

Conservation headlands

In an arable landscape, chick-food insects live mainly on weeds within crops. In a modern farm, killing these weeds with chemical treatments, or killing the insects themselves with insecticides, disrupts the chick's food supply. A grey partridge chick eat up to 2,000 insects per day, and can starve if insects are not sufficiently abundant. This was highlighted by a study that found chick survival was a third lower in areas of extensive insecticide use than on areas with little or no insecticide use[57].

A conservation headland is established by treating the area around the edge of an arable field with fewer, selective herbicides and insecticides than the rest of the crop. It may also be drilled more widely, to increase the space between rows and use less fertiliser. This allows game chicks to move more easily through it and makes space for more wildflowers and arable weeds in the outer strip of the field, which supports many more wildlife groups.

Establishing conservation headlands around fields increases the supply of chick-food insects. More than twice as many have been found in conservation headlands compared to headlands sprayed as normal[52]. This plentiful food supply can improve chick survival, and support larger brood sizes[52,63,79]. For example, a study of grey partridge chick survival on farms in East Anglia showed that survival rose from 23% on fully sprayed fields, to 39% in areas with conservation headlands, making the difference between population growth and decline[54,80].

Game cover crops

Food for adult birds can be provided by game cover crops. Choosing crops that retain their seeds and grains through the winter, and using a mix of different species can provide food at different times, providing a steady food source over the winter months.

The type of crop planted in game cover strips varies widely, and can range from those such as maize, which has limited conservation benefits, to specifically formulated wild bird mixes, which are designed to benefit a wide range of birds and are sometimes tailored to support particular species. The type of crop is influenced by what the keeper wants that strip to provide – foraging cover or winter cover.

Game cover crops are often treated with little or no insecticides, and therefore can also provide areas where insects are abundant, contributing to the overall effort to provide sufficient chick-food insects. Where nesting cover is provided, game cover crops are usually planted next to this, for example alongside a beetle bank or hedgerow, so that the hen can take her brood there to forage when they leave the nest. Game cover crops providing food and shelter for adult birds are usually sited along the edge of fields, next to woodland or hedges to give easy access to the resources they provide, and allow the birds to move around the countryside in safety.

Can birds of prey benefit from game management?

Birds of prey may threaten the viability of gamebird management because of predation. At the same time, it has been suggested that a wide range of raptor species can benefit from game management due in part to the abundance of prey including small mammals and wild farmland birds on shoots. In his 2012 book, *Partridges. Countryside barometer.*[39], the late Dr Dick Potts writes:

"In the recent past, nothing has divided bird protection and shooting lobbies more than their differing attitudes to raptors.
Yet, in the future, raptors could be the glue that binds the two lobbies together. Raptors need food and with modern agriculture there is less and less food for wildlife every year, except where gamebirds thrive."

© Marlies Nicolai/GWCT

A sight you might see on shoot day: A beetle bank provides a corridor through the centre of the field through which birds can move more safely © GWCT

Winter cover crops: for shelter

What are winter cover crops?

Areas in which gamebirds can forage and shelter from both predators, and severe weather. Plants which stand through the winter, and retain seeds through to spring are ideal winter cover. Some species, for example, maize, provide good cover until Christmas but then die off and collapse, leaving birds exposed if other species are not available nearby.

Some seed mixes include species which are suitable for winter cover as well as those which benefit chicks and adults earlier in the year. The placement of winter cover can be influenced by the layout of a shoot – cover in certain areas can be used to 'hold' birds which have travelled from their home wood to feed during the day at nearby sites, before driving them back, over the Guns.

Benefits to other species

Game cover crops have the potential to give great benefits to biodiversity on farmland. The extent to which they do this depends very much on the species or mix of species chosen, and this varies widely. The different mixes provide different benefits for both gamebirds and other species. The most diverse mixes are usually the most beneficial, with wild bird seed mixes being highly recommended to provide food throughout the winter, and preferred by a broader range of species.

For example, one study looking at game crops in Scotland (consisting of kale, triticale, mustard, wheat, oil seed rape and quinoa), recorded up to 100 times as many songbirds per hectare in game cover crops, compared to set-aside, stubble or conventional crops.

Game cover crops in this study attracted 21 bird species, including linnet, bullfinch, reed bunting, house sparrow, tree sparrow, song thrush, compared to 14 in set aside/stubble fields and only 11 in conventional crops[3].

© Peter Thompson

Another study looked at how many farmland birds were found on "winter bird crops" (WBCs) compared with conventional crops. This study of 192 farmland sites found that overall, bird densities were more than 12 times higher on WBCs. When the analysis was confined to the WBC species which the birds most preferred, this rose to 50 times higher[4]. These are just two of many studies that have shown the value of seed-bearing crops in winter[81].

The same profile of game cover crop species has also been studied in summer and shown to contain not only up to 80 times more birds than nearby conventional crops, but also 15 times more butterflies and 40 times more bumblebees[82]. When plants are considered, 90% more weed species were observed in game crops, some of which provide food for other bird species, but which also support more invertebrates[3,82].

The benefits of game cover crops to many farmland bird species are well established, with studies consistently demonstrating more than ten times as many birds found in game crops in winter, compared to control arable areas[2,4,83].

Game cover crops are widespread, with an estimate made from the PACEC survey of the shooting community published in 2006 suggesting that there are 93,000 ha of game cover crops in the UK[35]. Assuming this is near the true number, and using an estimate of two tonnes of seed per hectare from such crops, it has been put forward that 180,000 tonnes of seed per year could be provided from this source[84]. For game cover crops to fulfil their potential to support birds through the winter, they should not be ploughed in at the end of the season but rather should be left to stand and provide food through the hungry gap in the late winter and early spring, when many bird food sources are exhausted.

A well-managed hedgerow next to a field margin can provide protection from predators and the weather, nesting cover and foraging habitat round the edges of a field. © *Peter Thompson*

© *Peter Thompson*

Nesting cover: for safe nest sites

What nesting cover do gamebirds need?

Ideal partridge nesting sites are in thick grassy cover, often at the base of a field boundary or on low banks - slightly raised above the general field level. The site needs to be dry, sheltered and well concealed, with plenty of "residual" grass – dead grass from the previous year that helps with camouflage[39]. Pheasants will also nest in these sites, but in general prefer to breed along woodland edges with plenty of shrubby cover, particularly brambles[85]. Nesting attempts made later in the season tend to be in crops.

How do shoots provide this?

Hedgerow management

The UK hedgerow stock degraded in the second half of 20th century as farming policies encouraged their removal to optimise efficient mechanised farming methods. Many were retained during that period because of game interests. Hedgerows are very important for partridge nesting, in fact many studies have found that up to 75% of grey partridge nest in hedge bottoms when available[39]. However, the type of hedgerow is also important – for example, they should retain enough dead grass from the year before at the base to provide cover for a female grey partridge or wild pheasant sitting on a nest[61]. The modern approach of frequent hedgerow cutting reduces the amount of dead grass available, and we recommend that hedgerows should be cut every other year, rather than annually, preferably in late winter so that the berries produced by the hedge plants can be eaten by birds.

A good scheme for the farm as a whole is to cut one half or one third of hedges each year, ensuring that these are scattered across the farm rather than all in one area. This ensures that there are hedges at the right stage to suit the full range of wildlife needs spread across the whole area. Cutting every other year allows not only more berries, but also more flowers to develop on hedgerows. If cutting were to move to every three years, rather than every two, the quantity of berries would increase even further, meaning more winter food for wildlife[86,87].

Valuable hedgerows should also be protected from crop sprays, livestock browsing and cultivation. In order to support the broadest range of wildlife, the hedge should be made up of (mainly native) shrubs and trees including hawthorn, blackthorn and field maple. There is a requirement in the UK to maintain an uncultivated verge alongside a hedge without which it will support a less beneficial mix of plants on the ground. We also suggest that the margins alongside are not mown, unless scrub invasion is a problem. If the hedge base is dominated by nettle and other weedy species, they can be sprayed out and a cocksfoot-based mix can be sown to give good nesting cover for the future.

Traditionally, new hedges would have been allowed to grow fairly tall in most areas of the country, and then laid. This gives a tight hedge, which can then be allowed to grow. It is also a good way to restore hedges which have become spindly, but cutting and laying is labour intensive and therefore expensive. Another alternative, which is quicker and requires less skill, is to coppice. By cutting the plants off just above the ground, you encourage a group of stems in place of each one. Laying the cut tops as a dead hedge gives some short-term cover, and protects the re-growth from browsing by deer.

Did you know? Hedgerows support 1,500 different invertebrate species from 70 families, hawthorn alone has 209 species associated with it.

Benefits to other species

It has been estimated that a third of all Britain's plant species have been found in hedgerows[88], and a well-managed hedge is a wildlife haven year-round providing food and shelter in summer and winter. In general birds prefer hedges that most resemble their non-hedge breeding habitat[87]. So woodland species like blackbird, chaffinch and song thrush like tall bushy hedges with a few trees. Scrub species like linnet or yellowhammer prefer lower, wider and denser hedges. Open country species like grey partridge, whitethroat and corn-bunting will nest alongside hedges with good verges especially where low shrub or rank vegetation is locally scarce.

The hedge and the associated hedge base are one of the most important habitats on farmland for invertebrates. They provide overwintering habitat for beetles and spiders, whilst the plants themselves and the nectar, pollen and seed they produce are food for many different beneficial groups of insects including pollinators such as bumblebees, bird chick-food and the natural enemies of crop pests. In total hedgerows support over 1,500 different invertebrate species from 70 families[36]; hawthorn alone has 209 species associated with it[89].

Butterflies such as small tortoiseshell, peacock, red admiral, meadow and hedge brown, gatekeeper, orange tip, ringlet and several whites are commonly found alongside farmland hedgerows[90]. Occasionally other butterflies such as skippers and blues will take advantage on windy days of the shelter provided by hedgerows in otherwise open landscapes. Less common butterflies such the brown hairstreak or the brimstone will breed in hedgerows if they contain their blackthorn or buckthorn food plants.

Farmland hedges provide habitat for many mammal species including harvest mice, which use hedgerow verges to nest and dormice, which live in hedges with spring thorn flowers and late season fruiting tree and shrub species. Dormice also use hedges to travel from wood to wood. Predators such as shrews and bats commonly feed on insects along hedgerows. Greater and lesser horseshoe bats, for example, prefer taller hedges and will feed or glean directly from foliage.

Beetle banks

Beetle banks, invented by the GWCT, are raised strips across the middle of large arable fields, sown with a mix of tussocky grasses, and disconnected from the field edges to allow normal agricultural operations as well as discourage mammalian predators from hunting along them. This habitat provides ideal nesting cover for grey partridge, as well as overwintering sites for beneficial insects which can help control crop pests[91]. They are easy to establish and maintain, and cost little in terms of income foregone. Because beetle banks increase the number of beneficial insects in the field nearby, these can reduce the number of pests, for example aphids, in the crop[92]. Chemical treatments to the crops may be required less often because of the higher number of beneficial insects colonising from the beetle bank.

© Peter Thompson/GWCT

Benefits to other species

Beetle banks can be a haven for many species. Designed with partridge nesting in mind, they also provide overwintering sites for beneficial insects, which are found in higher numbers on fields with beetle banks. The possibility that they may allow fewer applications of pesticides can be a benefit for the wider environment and the farmer, as well as for the beetles themselves. Thousands of beneficial insects per square metre can be found on a beetle bank[91]. They also provide ideal nest sites for small mammals, for example harvest mice, which are found there in high numbers[71].

© David Kjaer

Shrubs or hedges planted along woodland edges on shoots provide shelter for pheasants and woodland birds. © GWCT

Woodland edge

An ideally designed woodland edge for wild pheasants to nest in provides shelter from the wind at ground level. This involves removing the lower branches and some trees to increase light in to the ground, allowing ground vegetation to grow. The provision of medium height trees and shrubs along the edge of the wood, and sometimes a suitable hedge further out should deflect wind up and over the wood itself[93].

Other areas can be used, and maintained in such a way that they are suitable for nesting. For example, ditches can be thought of as inverted hedge banks, and in some areas can offer valuable nest sites when left unmown.

Traditional crop rotations

Traditionally, the crop sown in a given field would change annually to achieve a balance between crops that deplete nutrients from the soil and those that allow it to recover. A good example of this is the inclusion of "grass leys" in the crop rotation, typically found on a mixed arable and livestock farm.

In this management, a mixture of grass and clover would have been sown at the same time as a cereal crop such as spring barley, and the two crops grow together with the grass and clover establishing itself under the taller barley. This is known as "undersowing", and allows a harvest during the first year of pasture establishment. After the development of herbicides, farmers still practising a grass ley rotation use a more limited range of herbicides during this year so that the clover can thrive; this allows other arable plants to grow and is good for biodiversity. When the barley is harvested, the ground is not ploughed and the grass crop has a head start - the field will be used for grazing or a crop of hay, typically for three years before bringing the field back into arable crop production. The absence of ploughing during this time is particularly beneficial to sawfly larvae, which overwinter in the ground as pupae and then emerge the following spring without being destroyed by agricultural operations.

Because clover is able to gather nitrogen from the air and "fix" it in root nodules, the breakdown of clover roots enhances the amounts of both nitrogen and organic matter in the soil. Therefore, clover acts as a natural fertiliser and contributes to soil health. Soil quality is enhanced after a grass ley period and the farmer plants a valuable crop such as winter wheat in the year following the rotational ley in the expectation of a high yield.

Rotational leys are one of the elements of traditional farming that historically sustained high numbers of farmland birds such as grey partridge and corn bunting, along with other wildlife species.

Benefits to hares of game management

The National Gamebag Census shows that the number of hares killed on contributing estates fell during the wars. NGC records indicate that hare bags in Edwardian times were about twice as big as in the early 1990s, and this is believed to reflect a genuine decline which largely happened in the 1970s. The decline was largely caused by the abandonment of traditional mixed farming in favour of modern methods. Hares like a patchwork quilt farmland similar to that required by grey partridge, which is why they often thrive on wild partridge projects.

These days they are a minor quarry species with voluntary moratoriums on shooting imposed where numbers are low. Hares have shown some recovery in recent decades partly thanks to shoots improving cover and grazing conditions and carrying out fox control. On livestock farms, cover is usually the limiting factor so game cover crops and strips of long grass are beneficial. On arable farms grazing is often poor in summer when the crops have lengthened. Shoots which provide more grass in the form of strips or patches of pasture can help here.

High numbers of foxes will limit hare numbers so predation control in the spring breeding period can be key to maintaining a sustainable hare population.

A Code of Practice for Brown Hare Management in England can be found at: **www.gwct.org.uk/managementfactsheets** and for advice on hare conservation, please visit **www.gwct.org.uk/haremanagement**.

© Laurie Campbell

Woodland management

Pheasants are birds of the woodland edge, which provides both shrubby cover and safe roosting sites on tree branches. Therefore, woodland management is an important part of management for pheasants, and the impact this has on the woodland habitat has been studied in some detail. Woodland also plays an important part of shaping the landscape for managing the birds on shoot days – driving pheasants between blocks of woodland and over the Guns.

How much UK woodland is there?

Thirteen percent of the UK's land area is woodland – 3.17 million ha. England is 10% woodland, Wales is 15%, Scotland 18% and Northern Ireland 8%[94].

How much of this is managed for pheasants?

14% of the UK's total woodland area is managed for pheasant shooting. In England, 28% is game managed, with 4% in Scotland and Wales[23].

What sort of management is done?

Firstly, it is important to note that game management appears to be one of the driving factors for landowners to retain and maintain woodland. Land managed for shooting contains on average ten times more woodland than that which is not managed for shooting[95], and this woodland tends to be better managed in terms of coppicing, and maintenance of glades and rides[1]. Game estates are also more likely to plant new woodlands, particularly broadleaf woodland (as opposed to conifer plantations)[95]. Studies suggest that game shooting encouraged landowners to retain existing woodlands, and to plant new ones, particularly during the period 1960s-1980s[96]. Game managers use a variety of woodland habitat improvements such as: sky-lighting; widening woodland rides; coppicing; thinning; increasing diversity at woodland edges; encouraging ground vegetation; and planting new areas of woodland.

What is sky-lighting?

Sky-lighting is creating openings in the canopy amongst mature trees, to reduce the tree cover and allow more light to penetrate to the lower levels. This is done by felling a group of trees, which creates glades. Game managed woods have between 2% and 7% less canopy cover[1].

What does this do?

The increased light that can penetrate to the ground encourages more vegetation at ground level. A GWCT study of 150 woods in southern England showed that woodland managed for pheasants have 31% more ground vegetation than non-game woods. The study also found 22-32% more birds in woodland managed for pheasants[1]. Edges and gaps in canopy cover are thought of as being hotspots of biodiversity in woodland, and of great conservation importance[97].

Woodland management for pheasants allows ground vegetation to grow, creating habitat for a range of species including rare butterflies and threatened woodland birds. © GWCT

What is thinning?

Thinning is another method of increasing the amount of sunlight that reaches the ground in woodland, by removing individual trees spread across the woodland and reducing the canopy density throughout, rather than taking out blocks to create large clearings, as with skylighting.

What are rides?

A ride is any linear opening or track within a wood, including all the area between the trees on either side[98]. They provide additional sunny areas for pheasants and other wildlife, as well as access through the wood. Rides have a gap in the canopy above wide enough to allow sunlight to reach the ground, and ideally at least one and a half times as wide at the canopy level as the trees are high, with a shrubby edge profile at ground level[85]. Rides increase the carrying capacity of the wood for pheasants when they are more than 30m wide, but do not provide additional breeding habitat, which needs to be true woodland edge that faces at least 70m of open ground[85].

Why are they used for shoots?

Wide, sunny rides give important extra edge habitat which is attractive for pheasants, providing areas where they can dry out and feed with their chicks. The gamekeeper uses rides for access to manage woodland and feed birds[93], and Guns are positioned within rides to shoot pheasants that fly over.

Why are they good for other biodiversity?

Rides and glades tend to support a completely different profile of plants and animals from the rest of the wood[98]. Sky-lighting, and the creation and maintenance of rides are both techniques which allow more sunlight to penetrate woodland, and lead to more plant growth at ground level. In fact, it is thought that the lack of vegetation at this understory level may be one reason for the recent decline of many woodland bird species[99]. Woodlands managed for pheasants have a more open canopy, denser herb layer and 5-58% more ground level vegetation[1]. Studies also show that they can have more birds and butterflies[1,6], In one of these studies, pheasant rides contained the highest numbers of 17 out of the 21 species of butterfly seen in the study[6].

© GWCT

What is coppicing?

Coppiced wood is cut periodically and the trees are allowed to regrow from the stumps. In an actively coppiced wood, an area of "underwood" – the trees that are coppiced – is cut each winter, and the wood usually also contains "standards" – mature trees that are left to grow (see inset).

Why is coppicing done?

Coppicing is a traditional technique that has been carried out in woodland for thousands of years to provide crops of young poles as well as larger timber, but is much less common in modern woodland. Between 1905 and 1967, the area of UK woodland managed by coppicing fell by 85%[100]. As well as game management, one of the main reasons for coppicing today is for conservation[100]. Actively managed coppice is very varied in structure, and therefore provides an attractive environment for many different species[101].

What effect does it have on woodland?

Coppicing keeps woodland more open and sunny, providing good habitat for many open-woodland species. Its loss over time has probably contributed to the lower amount of ground vegetation seen in less intensively managed modern woods[99,101]. In one study, in the later stages of the coppice cycle, the amount of light reaching the woodland floor in summer was only about 1% of that which reaches the ground in the open. This study also showed that, through the coppice cycle, the diversity of plant species at ground level increased for several years after coppicing, peaked at around 3-4 years and gradually declined after that[100]. Coppicing also affects other woodland species – some butterflies, in particular, require the open conditions of newly cleared woodland, ideally provided by coppicing[101].

Follow the Code

Shoot managers' obligation
"Shoot managers must endeavour to enhance wildlife conservation and the countryside."

© GWCT

Did you know?

A study found 22-32% more woodland birds in woodland managed for pheasants.

© Laurie Campbell

Supplementary feeding

Adequate food is a critical requirement for all animals, and gamebirds need plentiful sources of food if they are to thrive. As well as providing areas that are rich in food for birds to forage such as game crops, gamekeepers also provide additional food sources in the form of grain to support their birds through the winter and spring, when food is scarce. This is considered to be a central part of the gamebird management package.

Why do gamebirds need supplementary food?

Seeds and grains can be scarce on farmland in winter. Modern combine harvesters spill very little grain, and that which is left is often ploughed underground shortly afterwards. Overwinter stubbles, which used to provide a source of food, are left less often and are often sprayed after harvest to control weeds. The loss of livestock from many farming systems has also reduced the planting of fodder crop or the provision of animal food. which were useful resources for farmland birds[81]. In late winter (February/March) there is a period where very little seed and grain is available, known as the "hungry gap". This is a problem not only for gamebirds, but for many other seed-eating farmland birds as well[102].

Does supplementary food help gamebirds?

We know that higher densities of pheasants are found in winter in woodland where food is provided[103], and that estates that perform winter feeding have higher breeding densities than those that don't[104]. However, as recommended by GWCT guidelines, it is also important to continue this supplementary food to support gamebirds and other species through the spring hungry gap, rather than stopping it at the end of the shooting season on the 1st February.

How does spring feeding benefit gamebirds?

The GWCT ran a project in the late 1990s looking at the effect of spring feeding on pheasant body condition, density and breeding success. Feeding was continued until May/June on the study areas, and pheasants in these areas were compared to pheasants in areas where supplementary feed was only provided until the end of January. The study and reference areas were switched the following year, and compared again to make sure it was an effect of the feeding programme that was detected, rather than other differences between the study areas.

The results showed that in areas which provide supplementary food in spring as well as winter:

- Pheasant density was higher in April[105].
- More young were observed in September, although there was not a statistical difference[105].
- Females maintain their level of body fat from February through to April, whereas it drops by half in areas that do not feed in March-April[106].
- Females that lose a clutch lay a replacement clutch in half the time (average 15 days), compared to those who are not spring fed (average 31 days)[107]

Did you know?

The GWCT provides regular updates to feeding guidelines

Members of the GWCT can access the latest information about the best ways to feed your gamebirds and other farmland birds. For more information, visit **www.gwct.org.uk**.

© GWCT

How is supplementary food provided?

For both pheasants and partridge, grain is provided in hoppers, either along hedgerows, woodlands, game cover, or in open fields. The placement of feed hoppers may be affected by how well controlled the local rat population is. Supplementary feed should be provided throughout winter, and past the end of the season normally until the end of May to support released or wild gamebirds, as well as maximising biodiversity benefits.

Why does rat control affect the placement of hoppers?

Rats are known to visit feed hoppers, and encouraging and feeding a rat population is not desirable. In a recent GWCT study, brown rats made 17% of visits to feeding hoppers, but all of these were when feed hoppers were set along hedgerows[8]. When the hopper was moved, it took rodents longer than either gamebirds or songbirds to find the new location, so we recommend that feed sites are changed regularly. For more guidance, refer to the GWCT guidelines for successful gamebird and songbird feeding.

Benefits to other species

Breeding populations of many farmland birds are in decline, in part because more of these birds are not making it through the winter. It is thought that the smaller amount of seed available to them in modern farming systems contributes to this[81]. The "hungry gap" in late winter/early spring has been well described[102].

© GWCT

Provision of additional grain is well known to help farmland birds through the winter[65], and the limited studies specifically looking at gamebird feeding show that feeders are used by many species, including dunnock, blackbird and yellowhammer[8]. It seems that supplementary feeding can also help small mammals, as one study found more wood mice and bank voles near supplementary feed hoppers[7].

The importance of measuring success

Much of the discussion around shooting and the impact of management for it centre around biodiversity, and the possible effects that conservation measures can bring. In fact, the Code of Good Shooting Practice says that shoot managers must "endeavour to deliver an overall measurable improvement to habitat and wildlife". But how do you know what effect your efforts are having on the shoot? Are the birds and butterflies benefiting from your hard work, or is it not quite right yet?

The key is in the word measurable – to know wildlife is benefiting, you need to measure it, so monitoring the species you see on your farm or shoot is very important. Count a selection of the species that you have, in a consistent way, and you will know if they are thriving. If you have grey partridges you should certainly join the GWCT's Partridge Count Scheme (see chapter 10). GWCT also collaborates with the BTO over counts of British breeding woodcock, so if you have this species in summer you could join the count. You could also carry out breeding bird surveys along the lines of those carried out by the BTO.

Another useful tool is the Shoot Biodiversity Assessment, offered by the advisory department at GWCT. The advisors will thoroughly survey the shoot and the methods in place, examine the game and wildlife and how it is managed, and give a confidential report with an action plan for future improvement for the shoot, and the biodiversity.

Follow the Code

Measurable improvement
*"Shoot managers **must** endeavour to enhance wildlife conservation and the countryside."*

Management plan
"Shoot managers should prepare an appropriate, whole shoot management plan to ensure positive environmental benefit results from their activities and avoid excessive frequency of shooting over the same drives"

Ask the shoot

1. Do you plant cover crops that provide food and shelter for the gamebirds after the season has closed?

2. Do you plant a mix of cover crops, with other wild farmland birds in mind?

3. What do you do for pollinators?

4. What do you do to prevent rats round your feeders? Do you move them?

5. How late do you continue to put out supplementary feed?

6. How do you manage your woodland?

7. How do you manage your hedgerows for nesting birds?

8. What other wildlife benefits from the management of the shoot?

9. Have you had a biodiversity assessment?

10. If not, how do you measure improvement to wildlife on the shoot?

11. Can I see a copy of your shoot management plan?

12. How do you keep up with the latest information on game and wildlife management?

13. Are you a member of GWCT?

Generalist predators such as magpies and foxes are opportunists feeding on a wide range of food sources.
© David Mason

5. Predation management

Predation management is the attempt to reduce predation on species we value, either wild or domesticated. This plays an important part in gamebird management, as well as being used in other circumstances to protect livestock and wildlife. It is performed to varying degrees, using different approaches and methods by farmers, gamekeepers and conservation bodies across the UK, but the basic premise is the same: to protect a vulnerable species from predation.

What are predators?
A predator is any animal that preys on and eats other animals. The term applies to many species - from lions to spiders, species of fish and birds, domestic cats as well as humans. Some predators are very specialised and hunt only one prey species. Others, called generalist predators, are more opportunistic in what they eat, taking advantage of a wide range of food sources.

Left: © David Kjaer

How can predation be managed?

Both lethal and non-lethal approaches are widely used. Well-established non-lethal methods include scarecrows, habitat management, bangers and gas-guns, and the use of fences and electric fences to keep predators out.

Despite advances in non-lethal control methods in recent decades (e.g. manipulating behaviour, fertility control), there are still only three effective approaches to problem predators: scare away, fence out, or kill.

Predation control is often assumed to mean only the last of these, but in fact all three approaches are routinely used in game management, farming and conservation.

What is the aim of predation control?

The aim of predation control is usually to reduce losses to predation, especially during periods when the prey species are particularly vulnerable, for example the breeding season.

Where the main approach is lethal control, the aim is to reduce local predator numbers, or sometimes just to remove problem individuals. It is accepted that these animals will be replaced, either by others travelling from nearby areas, or by increased reproduction among those left. Because of this replacement process, any reduction in predator numbers is likely be temporary, and for a longer-lasting effect on predation, the control effort needs to be maintained or repeated frequently.

Control of invasive species

In general, the aim of predation control is to reduce losses to predation without impacting the conservation status of the predator, but exceptions are sometimes made. In the case of damaging, non-native predator species such as American mink in Britain, hedgehogs and rats in the Hebrides, the aim may be to eliminate them to avoid damage to native wildlife. In the case of hedgehogs, this has been done by moving them to the nearby mainland, where they are native and believed to be declining.

© David Kjaer

Predators and prey – the balance of influence

For much of the 20th century, the general view among scientists was that native predators mainly took old, sick or weak animals that would not have contributed much to the prey population anyway (this was charmingly called a 'doomed surplus'). Predator numbers were thought to be limited by prey numbers, rather than the other way around, and it was thought that predation would have little effect on prey population size. On the other hand, game managers in the UK believed that their control of predator numbers did benefit prey populations. This difference in views was sometimes put down to a difference in aims, with game managers interested only in boosting the number of harvestable birds in the autumn, while academics and conservationists were thinking of year-to-year population trends.

Evidence supporting the view that predation can and does impact prey populations began to build up with observations from the Sussex Study, a long-running GWCT study of farmland practices. Data from Sussex suggested that grey partridge nest losses were higher on farms that did not employ gamekeepers than those that did[46]. In his comprehensive 2012 book "Partridges", Dick Potts reviewed 74 studies of grey partridge nest predation performed across the world. Combining these studies showed that nest losses averaged 29% with a gamekeeper and 52% without, suggesting that predation control allows more successful nesting for partridge[39].

This does not now seem surprising, but it needed more rigorous science to change widely held opinions. The GWCT's Salisbury Plain Experiment was a large-scale field trial which studied whether legal predation control in spring and summer could improve breeding success and population growth for wild grey partridge[64]. Predation control was carried out on one study area, while a second similar area nearby acted as a comparison without predation control. After three years, predation control switched from the first area to the second. The predators targeted were fox, stoat, weasel, rat, carrion crow, magpie, jackdaw and rook.

This experiment showed unambiguously that controlling predators allowed 75% greater production of young. Despite shooting, this improvement carried over into successive years, so that spring breeding numbers increased by 35% each year and were 2.6 times greater after three years of predation control. Autumn numbers, before shooting began, were 3.5 times greater after three years. Clearly, this set of common predators was having a substantial impact on the local partridge population, and controlling them from March to September relieved much of the pressure[64].

Twenty years later, GWCT conducted a similar experiment on moorland in the north of England. The Upland Predation Experiment showed predation control led to benefits for breeding grouse, but also curlew, lapwing, golden plover and meadow pipit[108]. With predation control, these wading birds were able to breed well enough for population growth, an important threshold that was not reached in the absence of predation control.

The effect on the curlew population was marked – in the absence of predation control, curlew numbers were dropping by 17% per year. When legal predation control was implemented, curlew numbers rose by 14% per year (after a lag period as the new chicks reached breeding age)[108]. We have calculated that the low breeding success seen in this experiment on moors where predators were not controlled could lead to a drop in lapwing and golden plover numbers of 81%, and curlew of 47%, over ten years. This prediction has not yet been tested, but studies have shown higher curlew density on keepered moorland[109].

It is important to understand one thing in particular about generalist predators, which is that they use a wide range of different food sources. This can mean that, even for an individual predator, the "problem" part of its diet – the prey species that man values, may make up only a very small part of its food. Breakfast, lunch and dinner may be rabbits, but if the mid-morning snack is grey partridge or lapwing, a conflict can arise. This was shown in the Salisbury Plain Experiment, where predation had a substantial impact on grey partridges. All the evidence suggested foxes to be the most important predator. However, if we calculate the food requirements of all the foxes in the area, all the partridges killed in the experiment could only have provided about 2% of their diet. By far the main component of their diet, the staple food source, was rabbit and to a lesser extent hares: together rabbits and hares provided 85% of fox diet.

Can predation control reduce predation on pheasants?

We know that without predation control, reared pheasants can rapidly fall prey to predators following release, notably foxes[110]. It might be expected that, as with wild grey partridge and other ground-nesting birds, predation control would alleviate this and predation would be lower. However, the benefits of predation control for released birds have been surprisingly little studied.

One GWCT study showed that of reared grey partridges released as part of a reintroduction programme, survival rates were higher at the study site with predator control than at the study site without[67]. For pheasants breeding in the wild, predation is the most common cause of nest failure, accounting for 68% of losses in a GWCT study[29]. During the incubation stage, nest survival rates in areas with high predation control effort were almost double those in areas with low predation control effort. The main predators were foxes and crows[25,29].

Does predation control have wider conservation benefits?

Many studies have now shown that predation control conducted primarily for gamebirds can benefit other wildlife species, including: lapwing[111], blackbird[112,113], song thrush[113], dunnock[113], curlew[108,114], golden plover[108] and brown hare[28]. For this reason, predation control is also used by a range of organisations on nature reserves across the country.

Follow the Code

Shooting predators
"When shooting foxes, or other predators, suitable rifles, shotguns and ammunition should be used and only at ranges that ensure rapid despatch"

Displaying carcasses
"Shoot managers should not display carcasses. It serves no useful purpose and will offend other countryside users."

Keeping records
"Accurate records of pest and predator control carried out should be kept"

Exclusion fencing can be costly and have practical limitations. © *Andrew Hoodless/GWCT*

Does predator exclusion fencing work?

In some circumstances, exclusion can be helpful. For example, pheasant poults held in release pens are protected from most mammalian predators by a fence, often with electric fencing outside it. Scaring devices are sometimes added.

Wild prey can also be protected by exclusion fencing, if they occupy a relative small area. For example exclusion fencing can increase breeding success for lapwing[111,115]. However, the literature shows mixed results. Very small exclosure cages placed around individual nests can also be helpful, depending on the prey species protected and the predator species involved. For example, in one study lapwings appeared to benefit from such cages, but there was increased predation on incubating redshank. This was thought to be because redshank tend to stay on the nest until a predator is very near, then suddenly flush, at which point the cage becomes an obstacle to the escaping bird[116].

When the prey species is spread across a large area, or is mobile and will travel out of the protected area, exclusion may not work. In such circumstances, it can be more effective to reduce the predator population through lethal control. For example, a recent project to protect curlew nests in Shropshire and the Welsh Marches erected exclusion fencing around three nests. Of 21 nests studied, these three were the only ones to successfully hatch chicks; however no chicks survived to fledge, mainly because of predation once they were mobile enough to leave the fenced area[117].

Exclosure cages may help to protect groundnesting birds, but chicks are still vulnerable to predation once hatched © Andrew Hoodless/GWCT

There are several problems to be considered with fencing. There is a trade-off between the risk of fencing being breached by predators, practicality with other land uses and cost. This is increased with larger fenced areas. It may be too expensive to exclude small predators such as weasel, stoat, polecat, hedgehog; or those that climb, such as cats. There are typically weak points (e.g. corners, straining posts, and gateways) where predators can learn to gain access. It can be difficult or impossible to fence wetland areas with a variable water level, or where entry routes are exposed by low tides.

On the other hand, where the ground is very dry, it can be impossible to establish an earth for electric fencing. With good fencing, breaches may be very rare, but they can be catastrophic when they do occur. This is particularly true of electric fencing, where some individual predators seem to learn to tolerate the pain for the sake of the reward.

Exclosures also make vegetation management difficult because they can also prevent the free movement of wildlife, for example keeping out wild animals such as deer, while the handling and care of domestic livestock becomes much more laborious and time-consuming. It is generally considered uneconomic and impractical to fence even small pheasant release pens against aerial predators; so for wild ground-nesting birds, egg and chick predation by avian predators cannot be prevented by exclusion.

Are all individual predators problematic?

Animals are as varied as humans, and different individuals display different behaviours. Sometimes, problematic behaviour is shown only by certain individuals. For example, the clumped nature of fox predation on lambs suggests the concept of individual 'rogue' foxes, and the hope that selectively removing these may resolve the issue.

On the other hand, some behaviours are common to all members of a predator species. All foxes are likely to take a nesting bird if they come across it. There's also the problem of identifying 'rogue' individuals unless they are caught in the act. The Victorian gamekeeper's use of poisoned eggs is rightly outlawed today, but could at least boast that it automatically targeted only egg-eating individuals. Therefore, the usual approach is to treat all members of the species as potential predators.

Which predator species are controlled?

The main targets of (legal) predation control are: fox, stoat, weasel, brown rat, crow, and magpie. Jackdaw and mink may also be controlled according to local need, as well as other recognised pests of agriculture or forestry like rooks and grey squirrel. What all these species have in common (besides being known predators of gamebirds) is that they are all successful species, widespread and common in our modern landscapes.

Does predation control need to be performed all year round?

No, but the optimal strategy will vary from place to place. Wild gamebirds are particularly vulnerable to predation during the nesting period. To protect sitting hens, their eggs, and chicks, this is the time when predation pressure needs to be minimised. The ideal timing of control effort to achieve this depends on local circumstances. Lethal control has only a temporary effect until the animals removed are inevitably replaced. Because of this, winter culling will be largely irrelevant by spring, and it will be necessary to use methods that can be maintained through the spring and early summer.

As the greatest benefits for wildlife are generally seen when predators are controlled during spring, when many species are breeding[64,108], during the Salisbury Plain Experiment[64] the following predation control plan was used:

- Corvids (crows, rooks, magpies, jackdaws, jays) are egg predators and actively look for nesting birds during spring. Control was concentrated on the period from the end of March, through April and May.
- Small ground predators, such as rats and stoats, take partridge eggs and can also kill the sitting hen. These were controlled using tunnel traps through March to July.
- Foxes kill adult hen partridges during incubation, and were controlled mainly by shooting with a rifle focused on the end of May through June, but with some effort year-round.

A reared bird shoot whose business depends on the survival of released birds through the shooting season will prioritise control of predators, particularly foxes, during late summer and autumn to protect poults in and dispersing from the release pen. Because this is also the time of year when young foxes disperse, looking for territories, replacement will be rapid, and effort must be maintained. Very often this effort is then eased off in spring and summer when rearing-field duties demand time, so the benefit for wild game and other wildlife is small.

© Maurice Pullen

The GWCT's Salisbury Plain Experiment showed unambiguously that controlling generalist predators allowed 75% greater production of young wild grey partridge.

What is effective predation control?

Effective predation control reduces predation enough so that the prey species can benefit. Therefore, the important thing to consider is not how many foxes/crows/stoats have I removed, but rather how many remain, and what impact are they having?

This requires two things – a sustained effort, at the appropriate time of year to make sure the nesting season is covered, but also ongoing in future years, to maintain the benefit in the longer term. As predators that are removed will leave empty territories and available resources, others will inevitably replace them, so the effort must continue. It is important to understand that the aim is not to produce a long-term reduction in predator numbers overall, but to relieve the pressure for game and wildlife in the area at sensitive times of year. It must be expected to repeat this year on year.

If predation control is performed at too low a level to benefit the prey species, not done at their most vulnerable times of year, or not continued, it will be ineffective, and arguably unethical.

Pest control

A topic related to predation control, which in practical terms can be considered an aspect of the same activity, is pest control. Some wildlife can and do cause problems to many in the wider countryside, and control by gamekeepers can help contribute to overall control. At the estate level, the gamekeeper is usually required to manage pests as well as predators.

Which species are controlled as pests by gamekeepers?

This will vary from shoot to shoot, but typical species might include: rats, grey squirrels, rabbits, pigeons. When brown hares become very numerous – which they can easily do when predators, and especially foxes, are controlled[13] – they can do significant damage to growing crops, and it may be necessary to control their numbers too.

What about deer?

Deer can cause considerable damage to woodland when the population is unmanaged. Carefully planned deer management protects young trees, can improve the health of the herd and can improve biodiversity by protecting the woodland understory.

Why do gamekeepers target these species?

Rabbits, deer and pigeons can cause damage to both commercial and game crops. Rabbits, deer and grey squirrels can cause damage to woodland. Rats and grey squirrels can cause damage to feeders, eat supplementary food intended for gamebirds and eat birds' eggs.

Gamekeepers help to keep pest such as rats under control, which benefits wildlife in the wider countryside. © GWCT

So are there fewer pests on shoots than elsewhere?

This has not been studied, so we don't know. Game management activities do have the potential to favour some pest species, as well as to control them. For example, a low number of foxes and stoats can lead to increased rabbit populations, and man must also step in to control them[118].

During the breeding season, grey squirrels can predate songbird eggs.
© *Nigel Housden*

Provision of supplementary food for gamebirds can also help rats and squirrels, requiring extra control effort and care in how the feed is provided. Game strips provide cover which can favour rats as well as gamebirds. It's important to balance these effects to ensure that the conservation benefits of a well-run shoot are not lost.

Follow the Code

The Code applies to pest species
"The Code is primarily addressed to shooting 'game', but many of the principles apply equally to pest species including pigeons, crows rabbits and grey squirrels."

Is predation more of a threat now than in the past?

In lowland Britain changes in land-use, especially the intensification of agriculture, have made the countryside more challenging for wild ground-nesting birds. The chicks of many of these birds depend on insect food being abundant, which is now scarcer than it was in the past. As a result, these populations are breeding less well than before the 1960s. While we can restore a little of this former habitat through agri-environment schemes, these represent only a tiny part of what has been lost. This in itself leads to fresh problems, for example, field edge strips can both concentrate prey and channel predators along them[119-121]. Lack of connectivity increases the risk of local extinctions, so a fragmented population is far less robust than a connected one. Some prey species may be more vulnerable to predation now than they were in the past.

A range of factors has led to an increase in fox numbers since the 1960s. © David Mason

Are predators more common now than in the past?

Evidence about predator numbers is not as concrete as you might expect. Birds are well monitored by annual survey schemes set up by the British Trust for Ornithology, and for most species these extend back to 1962. Since 1995, mammals seen during the same surveys have also been recorded, and this provides a valuable back-up to other schemes for monitoring mammals.

The only longer-term dataset is the GWCT's National Gamebag Census, which records numbers of mammalian and avian predators killed ('bag data') on a self-selecting sample of shooting estates. When data become available from old sources, such as game record books, these are added retrospectively, so for a very few estates we have data from the early-Victorian era. The more systematic yearly data collection is carried out by questionnaire, and included predators only from 1961.

NGC data show a steady increase in fox bags from 1961 to the mid-1990s, but it is important to remember that bag data are ambiguous. A rising trend in the number of foxes killed could reflect: more foxes; greater effort; more effective methods or (paradoxically) an ineffective strategy where more individuals are taken from a larger population that is not under control. Predator bags are also affected by changes in legislation governing control methods (e.g. Wildlife & Countryside Act 1981, Hunting Act 2004); or technological improvement (e.g. thermal imaging).

Figure 6: Fox index from NGC bags
(1961-2013)

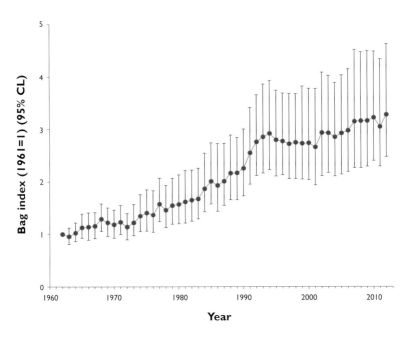

However, it seems likely that the striking rise in fox bags on shooting estates since 1961 is at least partly due to a real increase in the fox population, which in most cases will lie outside the shoot itself. This is also the period when foxes established populations in urban areas throughout the country, but we don't know the effect this has had on rural areas.

Over the years for which both NGC and BTO data are available (1995-2009), there is no statistically significant difference in the suggested trend for fox numbers: both suggest little or no change during this period. So overall, it looks likely that the UK fox population is higher than it has been historically, but has been fairly stable over the last 20 years. Broadly, the bags of fox, stoat, carrion crow, magpie are currently (in 2018) at levels 2-3 times higher than in the early 1960s, but the dynamics differ between species within that period and in different regions.

What do the lines on the graph mean?

Figures indicate the estimated size of the cull each year relative to 1961, after taking out sources of bias. We are 95% certain each un-biased cull estimate lies within the range covered by the vertical lines. Thus, the average bag from the mid-1990s to 2010 was most likely 3 times what it was in 1961; but it could have been between twice and four times the 1961 level.

Why have some predators become so common?

There are two angles on this, both of which are believed to be important. The first considers the 'top-down' regulation of predator numbers by bigger predators. Historically, humans eliminated top predators (wolf, bear, lynx) from Britain to benefit livestock farming. This would have released smaller predators (notably fox) from the pressure exerted by top predators, and may have allowed their numbers to rise. In the 19th century, gamekeepers effectively replaced the role of these top predators in limiting the middle predator populations; but following each of the two World Wars the number of gamekeepers employed to protect gamebirds fell dramatically (see figure 7 overleaf).

Since then, as far as we can tell, the numbers of generalist predators have risen, plateauing recently at higher numbers than were seen historically. However, during the same post-war period, the numbers of some food species such as wild game and others have declined. So clearly higher predator numbers must be supported by other food sources.

Figure 7: Gamekeepers in the UK
(1871-1971)

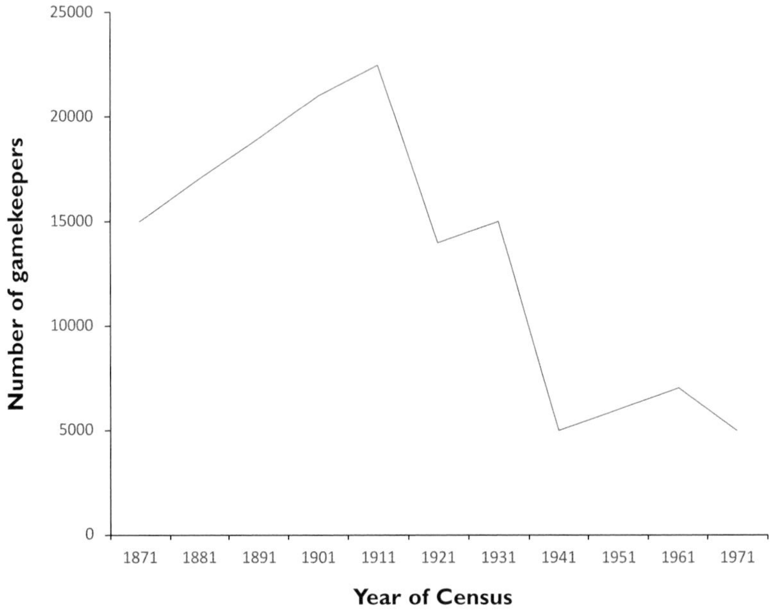

This figure shows the decline in the number of gamekeepers, as recorded in Census records between 1871-1971. From the 1981 Census onwards, the category of gamekeeper was grouped under agriculture, so there is no longer any official measure of professional gamekeeper numbers.

The other angle considers the resources that - in total - support predator populations. If a predator species has become more common, the food resources must be there to support the increased numbers. In a few thousand years, man has changed Britain beyond recognition, and the species that are successful today are those that can benefit from the conditions this has provided.

Agriculture, livestock and poultry farming, introduction of non-native prey species like the rat and rabbit, game management, road kills and the waste associated with all human settlements have created substantial food sources which these species have been able to use. Some (e.g. fox, magpie) now also have strong populations in urban areas, but we don't yet know the impact this has on adjacent countryside.

Whatever the reasons, in the modern world, many generalist predators thrive to the extent that they can seriously impact on the status of a range of vulnerable species, especially ground-nesting birds, such as red and black grouse, lapwing and curlew. For example, a large European study has shown that 65% of curlew nests observed between 1996 and 2006 were destroyed by predation[122].

Do shoots support high local predator populations?

It has been suggested that where large numbers of gamebirds are released for shooting, or where wild gamebirds are managed at very high densities, the increased supply of prey could provide easy food for predators such as foxes, supporting a higher number or boosting their reproductive rate. Of course if gamebird releasing is accompanied by rigorous predation control this could not happen; but the demands of gamebird rearing compete for the keeper's time in spring and summer.

This is an important question to consider, but at present few pieces of the jigsaw to answer it are available. A recent review of the effect of gamebird management examined seven studies, which found both positive and negative effects, but the majority were not significant. It concluded that "Overall, the evidence for a negative impact of gamebird releases on non-game species is not compelling, though appropriate large-scale experiments are absent"[123].

The use of Larsen traps in springtime helps to protect songbirds from corvids © GWCT

Focus on: Larsen Trap

Corvids are a family of birds that include crows, rooks, magpies and jackdaws. They are widespread across the UK and make use of many different food sources, one of which is predation on the eggs and chicks of other birds. This can have a serious impact on the nesting success of some species, including waders, gamebirds and some songbirds. Because these corvid species are so numerous, and because of the damage they can do to other birds, livestock and crops, it is legal to control their numbers under General Licences.

Until the late 1980s, control of corvids was a problem because cage traps were perceived to be very much less effective than poisons like alpha-chloralose, which, though illegal, were still being widely used. The GWCT were concerned about such illegal practices and, in investigating possible humane alternatives, became aware of a Danish cage trap called the Larsen trap. This trap alone had been credited with achieving a reduction in magpie numbers throughout Denmark. The design allowed the use of a "call-bird" of the target species in a separate compartment to attract other corvids into the trap.

GWCT scientists ran a small trial of Larsen traps under a special licence, showing that they were highly effective in general, but were ten to fifteen times more effective when a decoy-bird was used[124]. They realised that this was because of the highly territorial behaviour of breeding birds. It meant that effective control could be achieved within the critical time of year for gamebirds, with just a few of the conveniently-small traps moved around among different territories. It promised a far more focused approach to corvid control. However, the use of a decoy, and the small dimensions of the trap, contravened different aspects of UK wildlife law and would need to be specifically permitted.

GWCT approached the Nature Conservancy Council (now NE, SNH, NRW, DAEDS) regarding possible authorised use of Larsen traps. The NCC granted a licence for a wider trial in which registered gamekeepers could use Larsen traps in return for catch data[125]. This confirmed the overall effectiveness of the trap, and showed that selectivity as well as effectiveness was greatly increased through the use of a decoy bird. Of over 10,000 birds captured, only 1% were non-target species, and these could be released alive and unharmed.

The NCC decided that it would be a positive step to permit the control of corvid birds using Larsen traps, by issuing a General Licence. Today, General Licences issued by all the devolved administrations permit the control of corvid birds for specific reasons (e.g. protection of crops, wildlife conservation, public health), dictate which traps may be used, and impose conditions for maintaining the welfare of decoy birds.

Follow the Code

It is an offence to destroy, birds and their nests or eggs

"With certain exceptions, e.g. control under the authority of a general licence, it is an offence to intentionally kill, damage or destroy birds, their active nests or eggs."

Predation control and the law

The majority of predatory mammal and bird species in the UK are protected by law, but UK legislation treats mammals and birds differently. The following is a summary of the legal framework in May 2018.

Birds
For birds, the bottom line is that all species are protected, and killing them would ordinarily be illegal; but control of some species for which there is no current conservation concern (e.g. carrion crow, magpie, rook, jackdaw, jay) is permitted for specified purposes through General Licences.

Mammals
Mammals of conservation concern are protected by inclusion on one of the Schedules of the Wildlife & Countryside Act 1981, or by specific Acts (e.g. seals, badger). In some cases, protection applies only to certain methods of control. In general, mammals have less protection under UK law than birds do. So although some mammalian predators are strictly protected (e.g. pine marten, otter, hedgehog, polecat, badger) and may only be killed or taken under a special licence, others may be killed without any licence, while a few are protected against certain methods. The mammalian predators that may be killed without any licence are fox, grey squirrel, brown rat, stoat, weasel, and mink. However, the methods allowed are regulated (see below).

Licences
There are various kinds of licence, ranging from individual licences allowing a named operator to kill a specified number of birds; to General Licences, which permit anyone to kill certain species, using methods that are specified in the licence, for specific purposes including conservation of wild birds, protection of feedstuffs or crops, and prevention of disease. All licences are time-limited.

General Licences, issued separately in England, Wales, Scotland and Northern Ireland, are usually reviewed at 1 or 2-year intervals, and it has been normal for them to be renewed automatically. The activities permitted by a General Licence apply to anyone: individuals do not need to apply, although it is a condition of some General Licences (e.g. trapping corvid birds in Scotland) that you register your name and contact details. You must in any case be aware of what the General Licence says. General Licences differ slightly between England, Wales, Scotland and Northern Ireland, and details can be found on the websites of Natural England (NE), Scottish Natural Heritage (SNH), Natural Resources Wales (NRW), or the Department of Agriculture, the Environment and Rural Affairs (DAERA) in Northern Ireland. Licence conditions may change on review/renewal. Organisations such as the GWCT, BASC and the NGO will normally make their members aware of any changes, but it's up to you to keep up to date.

The use of snares is limited by the Wildlife & Countryside Act 1981.
© GWCT

Methods

Lethal control methods are regulated in various ways. Certain methods are forbidden by the Pests Act 1954 or the Wildlife & Countryside Act 1981. Kill traps are regulated under the Pests Act through occasional Spring Traps Approval Orders, whose details again vary between the devolved administrations. The use of snares is limited by the Wildlife & Countryside Act 1981. Use of firearms is regulated by the police under firearms legislation. The use of dogs is regulated by the Hunting Act 2004. The Animal Welfare Act 2006 applies to any wild animal brought into the control of man; this includes animals caught in traps, or rendered into hand as a result of shooting.

Protected species

Little research has been done into the impact that protected predators may have on wildlife or game, the priority for GWCT being to focus on common predators that were likely to be having the biggest impact.

It is also a very sensitive issue, because the poor conservation status of some species by the middle of the 20th century (e.g. buzzard, red kite, polecat, pine marten, wildcat) was attributed to their control by gamekeepers during the previous 150 years[59].

Several of these species (e.g. polecat, buzzard, red kite) have recovered well, and some other protected species (e.g. badger, sparrowhawk, goshawk) have prospered during the last half century. Concerns around their impacts on prey species have begun to reappear.

It is crucial that such issues are clarified through good science and debate, maintaining respect for existing law, but seeking change where evidence shows it to be appropriate. Illegal actions by a few cause immense reputational damage to the game management sector, and must be condemned by those wishing to maintain a countryside rich in game and other wildlife.

Applications can be made under existing law to control such species, where there is a sound argument for doing so and there is no other satisfactory solution. These are considered by the countryside agencies (NE, SNH, NRW, DAERA) on a case-by-case basis. If granted, a licence is issued to a named individual, with conditions, and limited in time and scope. These licences are anonymous.

Several such applications have been made in recent years to control buzzards, notably because of their impact on young pheasants and red-legged partridges in and around release pens, but also for predation on brown hare leverets, skylarks and lapwings, and to date four licenses have been granted. This avenue provides a legal route for those who are experiencing a genuine problem caused by a protected species, where alternative options have been explored. There is no valid reason for breaking the law and removing these animals without a licence. The GWCT strongly condemns illegal predator control, which risks bringing game management into disrepute.

Ask the shoot

1. What non-lethal methods of pest and predation control do you employ?

2. What time of year do you carry out fox control?

3. If you use snares, do you use the GWCT approved snare and has the person setting the snare had the appropriate training?

4. What are you doing for brown hares?

5. Do you perform deer management and squirrel control in your woodland?

6. Do you keep records of all pest and predation control carried out?

7. If you run a Larsen trap what time of year do you use it?

8. Are you consistent in the level of pest and predation control activity you undertake each year?

9. Is all your predation control legal and/or licensed?

Focus on: Fox Snare

While all lethal predation control is controversial, the use of snares is particularly so, with many attempts to outlaw them through Private Member's Bills.

When correctly used, they can be a very effective and selective way to catch foxes with a low risk of causing poor welfare. The difference between good and bad use lies partly in the choice of equipment used, but most of the difference comes from operator practices. Given both good equipment, for example the redesigned GWCT breakaway snare, and careful operating practice, fox snares have been shown to meet international humaneness standards for restraining traps.

The intention of modern snares is to catch and restrain the fox until it can be humanely dispatched by shooting. The mistaken public perception is that the snare strangles the animal.

This public understanding of snares is fuelled by images of scenarios that have clearly caused suffering. However, these are almost entirely avoidable, by following the Code of Practice (issued separately in England, Wales, and Scotland). In Scotland, it is mandatory to follow the CoP, but this is not the case in England and Wales. Here the CoP outlines basic legal requirements, but compliance with its additional recommendations is voluntary.

The recommendations of the CoPs are based on years of research by GWCT, and we know that they spell the difference between high-risk and low-risk operation. Our message on this is stark: those who use snares should aim for best possible practice, or expect to lose the technique.

The single most important point is to avoid setting snares where a captured animal could entangle the snare with some fixed object nearby. Injuries and death are almost exclusive to situations where animals have become entangled. A snare set under a fence line, close to a tree or bush, or next to a substantial anchor post, is highly likely to cause suffering, and this is avoidable.

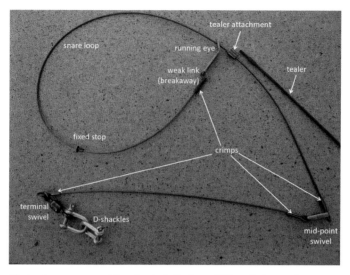

The breakaway snares catch and restrain the fox until it can be humanely despatched. © *GWCT*

Is it necessary to use fox snares? The majority of foxes killed in the UK are shot with a rifle, and the equipment available for this purpose has improved substantially in recent years with the wider availability of night vision equipment. However, shooting requires clear sight of the animal. For much of spring and summer – the key season for conservation of wild game and other wildlife – vegetation is typically taller than a fox. This is when snares have a unique advantage. Effective fox control at this time may only be possible given the use of snares.

You are unlikely to see fox snares in use during the shooting season, but they are commonly used around pheasant release pens in late summer/ early autumn. In this situation, extreme care needs to be taken to avoid entanglement.

For further information, including the Snaring Code of Practice and Snaring in Scotland, a practitioner's guide, see the GWCT website.

Follow the Code

Setting snares

"Snares should be set in accordance with the relevant code of practice for their use."

Resident woodcock are declining, whereas migratory populations are stable © Laurie Campbell

6. Other quarry species to look out for

Woodcock

The woodcock is one of the most esteemed of all quarry species. It has fascinated many sportsmen, not only because it is a challenging and difficult shot, but because it is a secretive and nocturnal migrant bird, whose elusiveness magnifies its appeal.

What is happening to woodcock populations in the UK?

The number of woodcock in the UK fluctuates widely throughout the year, because the population is made up of two distinct groups: those who breed here (resident); and those who breed elsewhere but migrate here to spend the winter (migratory). This distinction is important because the population trends are very different between the two sections of the population. The number of resident birds is declining, whereas migrant populations are stable[126–129].

What does this mean?

It means that the two sections of the population need to be thought of very differently from a conservation perspective. We need to focus conservation efforts on resident woodcock.

How many resident and migratory woodcock are there?

The latest estimate in 2013 suggests that there are about 55,250 males breeding in the UK in spring[127], but approximately 1.4 million individual birds here in winter[37]. We estimate that around 11% of the winter population are resident breeders.

Many shoots have shown voluntary restraint in response to falling resident woodcock numbers. © Steve Round

What is happening to the resident woodcock population?

Because the woodcock's breeding range has reduced by over 50% in the last 25 years, it was moved to the red list of Birds of Conservation Concern in 2015[130].

What does this mean?

The area of the UK where woodcock breed has reduced by half. These resident breeding birds are now in the highest category of conservation concern.

How are migratory woodcock populations faring?

Migratory woodcock mainly originate from Scandinavia, Finland, the Baltic states and Russia[131], and the available evidence suggests that these populations are stable[128]. Woodcock are considered to be of "least concern" at both the global and European level on the International Union for Conservation of Nature and Natural Resources (IUCN) red list[129].

What is causing resident woodcock declines?

This mysterious and cryptic species is difficult to study and we simply don't know all the answers, but a GWCT study recently submitted for peer-review prior to publication suggests a combination of[132]:

- More fragmentation of woodlands.
- Lower diversity within woodland due to changing woodland practices.
- Higher predation pressure.

What research is being done to understand woodcock?

The GWCT has performed a lot of research into woodcock ecology and conservation over the last 40 years. We still have many projects ongoing. We devised an appropriate survey method for breeding woodcock and pushed for national surveys with the BTO in 2003 and 2013, to quantify the size of the population and change in numbers[127,133]. We are studying their migratory patterns, habitat requirements and response to cold weather.

What UK habitats do woodcock prefer?

Breeding woodcock in the UK appear to thrive best with large, well-connected and heterogeneous woods and the presence of certain tree types, predominantly birch, combined with low predation pressure, lack of human disturbance and favourable weather conditions[132].

© Steve Round

Did you know?

The woodcock was moved to the red list of UK Birds of Conservation Concern in 2015 but is considered to be of "least concern" at both the global and European level.

Why is low predation pressure important for waders?

Like other waders, woodcock nest on the ground, which makes them vulnerable to a wide range of predators. Predation is one of the major factors influencing nesting success for many ground-nesting birds[64,134,135]. One example of this is the lapwing population in the Avon Valley in Hampshire. Many years of habitat management and low intensity farming have likely slowed declines, but the population is not yet recovering. Predation of nests and chicks has been found to be limiting population recovery in an otherwise suitable environment.

How does game management help breeding woodcock?

The management techniques employed on pheasant shoots can create suitable breeding habitat for woodcock. Predation control combined with woodland management, in particular encouraging understorey growth through coppicing and deer management, could benefit woodcock which nest on the ground.

Shooting woodcock

Why does the GWCT not support a statutory ban on shooting woodcock?

We do not believe that banning shooting will reverse declines in the long term, and a ban may prove counterproductive. Reversing the national decline of other quarry species, such as black grouse, has been achieved by working with shoots to maintain good habitat and protection from generalist predators alongside voluntary restraint. This approach has proven to be effective for the recovery of both black grouse and grey partridge. The shooting community has already responded to GWCT calls for people to show caution where woodcock are declining locally, and is working with us to create and maintain breeding habitat to promote local recovery. We would like to harness that interest to understand more about the species and ultimately try and reverse declines. There is nothing at present to suggest that legal protection would help stem the decline.

But would a ban not help reverse population declines in the long term?

We do not believe that a ban on woodcock shooting would help recover our resident woodcock for three reasons:

1. There is already an indication, at a national scale, of a reduction in hunting pressure over the last 20 years, with many people deciding voluntarily that they will no longer shoot woodcock. This suggests that another factor, such as change in habitat quality or predator abundance, is primarily responsible for driving the decline.

2. A ban may remove the motivation for some landowners to manage their woods in ways that maintain suitable habitat for woodcock.

3. Parts of western Britain have no history of breeding woodcock, but host large numbers of migrants, so shooting in these areas does not put residents at risk except during cold spells when residents might move south and west. In these areas, woodcock can be an important quarry species in its own right.

Do we know how many woodcock are shot in the UK?

The only estimate we have is from the same survey in 2014, suggesting that 160,000 woodcock were shot in the 2012/13 season[12]. This is data from one year only, and we do not know how reliable it is.

How many of those shot woodcock were residents?

We don't know for sure, but a PhD study supervised jointly by the GWCT and the University of Oxford recently analysed the feathers of 1,129 birds across the UK, and concluded that less than 2% of shot woodcock were residents[136].

So how many resident woodcock are shot each year?

This is also not known. If we extrapolate this 2% figure to the 160,000 woodcock shot in the season 2012/13, it would suggest that 3,200 of those birds may have been residents. However, we do not know if this is an accurate estimate.

Are migratory woodcock shot in the countries in which they breed?

Yes. There is an autumn hunting season in Scandinavia and short autumn and spring seasons in Russia. Evidence suggests that these populations remain stable[126,128].

© GWCT

How can we improve our knowledge of the impact of shooting?

There are several ways in which the impact of shooting could be assessed, and we have started this work with woodcock. One of the best ways of determining whether the mortality from shooting on resident populations is additive to natural mortality is through an experiment, but this will be difficult to carry out, and will need to be conducted over several years.

What has the shooting community already done to help woodcock?

The majority of research on woodcock, including the two national surveys that confirmed the scale of decline in our resident birds, has been funded by the shooting community through a desire to better understand the ecology of the species and ensure that shooting is sustainable.

How could further research help reverse the decline?

The GWCT has started to attach GPS tags to resident woodcock in order to better understand their breeding behaviour. Through following the precise movement of birds during the breeding season, we can develop a broader understanding of their complex habitat requirements, the common causes of mortality, including predation, and the effects of disturbance. This information can then be used to provide the best possible advice to those that manage our woodland.

How can shoots help recover resident woodcock numbers?

Habitat appears to have a significant influence on the rise and fall of resident woodcock numbers. The habitat requirements of woodcock vary with different stages of the life cycle. The mixture of woodland habitats, or the landscape as a whole, may have a significant effect on woodcock abundance. Shoots across the UK can help, by both gathering evidence about their habitat requirements and then by managing habitat suitable to support them.

Woodcock shooting guidelines

Why were guidelines for woodcock shooting produced?

Although it is unlikely that shooting is the main factor driving resident woodcock declines at a national level, we can't rule it out as a contributory factor locally. Shoots should do all they can to reduce any local impact. Therefore, in 2015 we published guidelines to reduce the impact of shooting on resident birds and we welcome their adoption by shooting organisations.

For more information, visit **www.gwct.org.uk/woodcockposition**.

What do these guidelines suggest?

We believe it would be prudent for those who intend to shoot woodcock to:

1. Improve understanding of local woodcock populations before considering shooting
2. Show restraint even where resident birds are absent
3. Shoot flight lines with caution
4. Curb shooting in freezing weather

How does improved understanding of local populations help?

A thorough knowledge of local quarry populations is always advisable when shooting. For woodcock, we advocate improving local knowledge about the presence and trend of resident breeders and the numbers of woodcock typically present at different times during the winter. For instance, on the east coast of Scotland the largest numbers of migrant woodcock are often present in November, whereas in southern England migrant numbers are typically highest in January. These local variations will influence when shooting is least likely to impact resident populations.

Why should restraint be shown when resident birds are absent?

Restraint when shooting woodcock makes sense even in areas where there are no local breeders, because we know from our satellite tracking and annual ringing of woodcock that the majority of migrant woodcock are extremely faithful to the same wintering site year on year[132]. Shooting these will therefore break this migratory link and is likely to lead to fewer woodcock being seen in that area in the future.

What does "shoot flight lines with caution" mean?

Flight lines are the regular routes used by woodcock to travel between woodland and nearby fields at dawn and dusk in winter. As several birds may exit a wood at the same point and follow similar, predictable routes, excessive shooting along them carries the risk of severely reducing the local population. We advise caution if flight lines are shot to reduce the risk of overshooting.

Why is shooting restricted in cold weather?

Woodcock feed mainly on earthworms and soil invertebrates, by probing the ground with their long bills[137]. Frozen ground therefore prevents them feeding easily, which is why they migrate to warmer countries to overwinter rather than staying at their breeding grounds. Feeding can also be restricted during cold spells in the UK (and some even temporarily travel further south and west to escape cold snaps). During such times, woodcock are at higher risk of starvation and probably predation, so every effort should be made to reduce additional mortality.

How is the weather monitored for shooting?

A network of 25 Met Office weather stations across the UK monitor weather daily. When more than half of these meteorological stations have recorded frozen conditions for seven consecutive days (determined from minimum air and grass temperatures, but allowing short periods of thaw), the country conservation agencies liaise with BASC who normally advise a period of voluntary restraint from shooting where appropriate whilst severe weather conditions last[138].

When does a mandatory restriction apply?

On the 13th day of frozen conditions, if more than half the relevant meteorological stations are still frozen, a case is presented to the relevant Secretary of State(s) requesting a suspension on waterfowl and wader shooting due to the severe weather. This comes into force at 00h01, two days after the case was presented, and will be widely publicised.

More details of the process are available at:

http://jncc.defra.gov.uk/page-2894.

Our current advice on shooting woodcock in cold weather

Recent research at the GWCT has shown that the average time for which woodcock can fast before starving to death is six days[139]. During most cold spells, woodcock are still able to feed by altering their behaviour and feeding in the middle of the day, when the ground is sufficiently thawed.

However, when the ground remains continuously frozen during day and night woodcock rapidly lose condition. We therefore advise stopping shooting woodcock after four days of continuously frozen ground. The birds should then be given a chance to recover for at least a week after the ground has thawed before shooting recommences.

Yes - woodcock can be shot when:

- The shoot has a good understanding of local woodcock populations –numbers of both breeding birds and migrants.
- There have been good numbers of migrant woodcock in the area.
- Restraint is practised even where resident birds are absent – overshooting might break the migratory link with the shoot.
- The area has no history of breeding resident woodcock that could be at risk, only migrants.
- Guns only shoot flight lines with great caution as there is a much higher risk of overshooting.

No – woodcock should not be shot when:

- Numbers have been low in the area and the impact of shooting may be greater.
- It's too early in the season and the first migrants have just arrived. Whilst every shoot will be different, generally we recommend not shooting woodcock before 1st December.
- A statutory cold weather suspension is in force.

The mysterious and much-loved woodcock can benefit from shoot management. © Steve Round

Woodcock facts

Despite usually being found in woodland, woodcock belong to the wader family - a group of birds most of whom spend parts of their life wading in the shallow waters of the sea, estuaries and lakes. They are referred to as "shorebirds" in America.

Woodcock are between blackbird and partridge in size. Typically 33-35 cm from head to tail, with a long slender bill of 6.5-8 cm. The plumage and size of males and females is very similar, preventing the sexes from being distinguished in the field, other than on the basis of behaviour.

The pattern and mottled brown colouring of their plumage provides excellent camouflage in undergrowth or against leaf litter and they can be almost impossible to spot on the ground[32].

When disturbed in woodland, woodcock tend to explode from the ground with a sudden audible burst of wing beats and jinking flight, whereas commuting flights between woodland and fields tend to be fast and direct.

During the breeding season, males make slower courtship or "roding" flights at dawn and dusk, which are accompanied by a distinctive call consisting of three or four low 'croaks' followed by a shrill whistle.

Woodcock prefer deciduous or mixed woodland for breeding, with clearings, glades or rides. Fairly moist, but not wet, soils are preferred, with suitable dry, warm resting places and wetter areas, such as springs, ditches and swampy patches for feeding. Woodcock do not tolerate disturbance well, so freedom from disturbance by human and dogs, but even pheasants and rabbits is preferred.

Like many waders, woodcock are migratory, breeding in one location and migrating to another for the winter months. In the British Isles, there is a small population of woodcock which is resident year-round and a much larger migratory population which breeds in Scandinavia, Finland, the Baltic States and Russia, and travels to Britain and Ireland for the winter.

Woodcock feed on the ground, eating mainly animal material, for example earthworms, insect larvae and beetles, but also some plant material and seeds, particularly if other food is scarce in winter. They probe with their bill, rather than scratching with feet as pheasants do[32].

Nests are a shallow depression on the ground, made by the female and often lined with a few dead leaves or dry grass. In woodland, they are often concealed beneath bramble or dead bracken but can be in relatively open locations near a fallen branch or base of a tree. Nests are occasionally located in fields, marshes or heathland, typically in rushes or heather. Egg laying starts in early March in the UK, with the peak during mid-March to mid-April. Clutches typically consist of four eggs, laid at intervals of 1-2 days, with incubation starting with the laying of the last egg and lasting for 21-24 days. When young hatch they are immediately mobile and can leave the nest, but appear to be helped with feeding by the female for the first 4-5 days. Chicks are capable of flight at 15-20 days, and independent of the female at 5-6 weeks[32].

Snipe

Another bird you might encounter on shoot day is the snipe. The small wader breeds locally across Britain but its current distribution is biased towards northern England and Scotland. The highest densities of birds are found on wet lowland grass that is subject to periodic flooding.

How many snipe are there in the UK?

The BTO estimates the British summer population was 76,000 pairs in 2009 and winter population 1million individuals in 2004/2005[37]. In winter, snipe come to the British Isles from Russia, Scandinavia and Iceland.

Why are the UK's breeding population in decline?

Snipe are classified by the IUCN as of Least Concern globally, but its breeding range in lowland Britain has declined steadily since the 1950s, which is one of the reasons for its amber listing[130]. Declines in the UK are probably due to wet meadow drainage, increased stocking rates and silage production. Breeding success is often poor because a high proportion of nests is lost to predators and many nests and chicks are trampled by livestock[173].

How many are shot?

The estimated snipe bag based on NGC returns in the 2004/2005 season was 64,000 and 100,000 in the 2012/13 season[174].

What is the difference between Jack snipe and common snipe?

Though both have similar colour plumage, Jack snipe are smaller than common snipe with a shorter bill. They are protected in England, Scotland and Wales and care must be taken not to shoot them accidentally, if in doubt, it is best practice to show restraint.

© David Kjaer

Snipe facts

Snipe are 26 cm in length with a 46 cm wingspan. They have a diet of invertebrates (insects, worms and snails) found on wet ground or shallow water and located by touch. Habitat includes lakes, bogs, marsh, grassland, heath, moorland and along streams. The first and only clutch of four eggs is laid in a nest on the ground around 30 April and the young take 20 days to hatch.

Because of its unpredictable flight when flushed, zigzagging and then flying off high, the snipe remains a highly prized quarry species, especially in Western Britain. The buzzing noise known as drumming is similar to the bleating of a sheep, hence the snipe's colloquial name heather bleater. It is produced by the wind whistling through its spread outer tail feathers and accompanies the snipe's distinctive territorial display on warm summer evenings[32].

© Laurie Campbell

Wildfowl

This chapter refers to the types of wildfowl shooting a Gun might encounter on a driven or inland rough shooting day and related habitat management. For guidance on coastal wildfowling and more detail on wildfowl shooting in general, see *The BASC Handbook of Shooting*.

Mallard

The mallard is the most familiar duck in the UK. It is easily recognisable and very adaptable, found in rivers, ponds, streams, wetlands and reservoirs across the country. Despite being so widespread and thought of as common, the population of mallard is actually falling in Britain recently and it is now amber listed because of these declines.

How many wild mallard are there in the UK?
It is difficult to know accurately, but estimates suggest there are around 60,000 to 145,000 breeding pairs in spring, who are joined in the winter by many more from Iceland and northern Europe – taking the overwintering population of wild mallard to around 700,000 individuals[37].

Can mallard be released?

Yes. Mallard can be reared using the same techniques as pheasants and partridge, and released. Mallard make up the vast majority of the ducks shot inland in the UK.

Is it done in the same way?

The process is very similar. Ducklings are raised in game farms – tending to be ones that specialise in duck – and are released at around 8-10 weeks to a pond on the shoot. This may be fenced to keep predators out, but if predation control is performed in the area it may not be needed. The main predators for mallard are fox and mink.

Follow the Code

Releasing mallard

"Duck must always be released into suitable wetland habitat, and in numbers which are appropriate to its carrying capacity"

"Wetland areas are particularly sensitive, and overstocking with reared birds must not be allowed to deter wild stocks or damage the habitat"

"Duck must be encouraged to become wild and shooting must not be undertaken until they have done so."

"Shoot managers should ensure that ducks have alternative water to which to fly."

Can releasing harm the local ecology?

As with pheasant release, it is important to recognise the possibility for environmental harm if mallard release is performed at too high a level in too small an area. Although the scientific evidence base is not as detailed or robust in this situation, experience highlights that the release of an inappropriately high number of birds can have a negative effect on the release pond itself and the wildlife that shares it.

Do the reared duck fly away?

Usually not. They tend to stay on the same pond, or move between nearby ponds if there are several in the vicinity, but will not travel very far. Wild mallard may join the released birds so numbers may grow through the year.

How many mallard are shot each year?

We don't know the total number with certainty. It is not compulsory to record or report the number of birds (or other game) you shoot, so we can only monitor the number shot by those who voluntarily send their information to the GWCT's National Gamebag Census (NGC). For more information about the NGC, what it can tell us and how it works, see chapter 10. Using NGC data combined with other sources, we have estimated that the total UK bag for mallard was close to a million in the 2012/13 season[24].

Figure 8: Mallard index from NGC bags
(1961-2011)

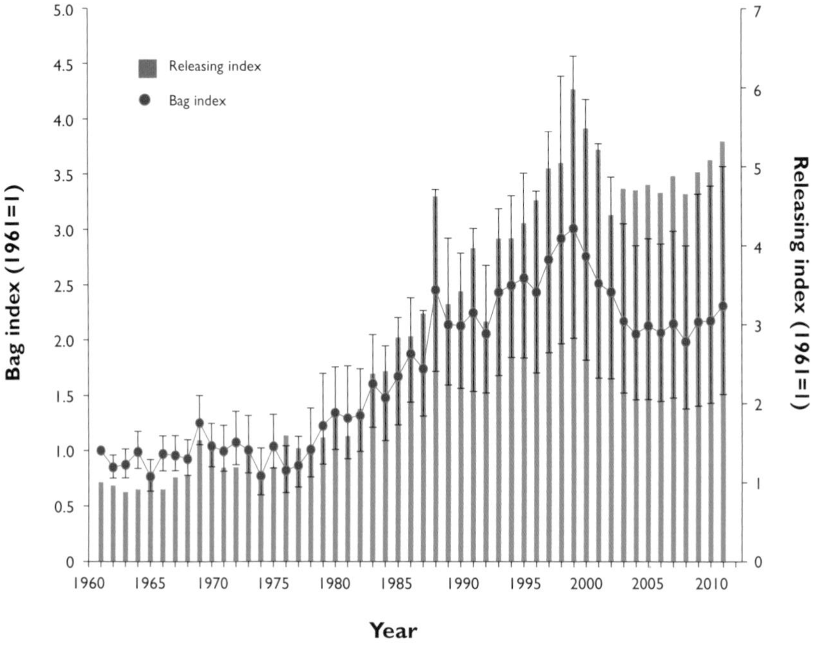

How many of these were released compared to wild?

We also don't know the proportions, as it is not possible to tell a wild from a released bird unless they are tagged. We do know that from those who send us their bag returns, approximately five times as many mallard were released in 2011, compared to 1961. The number of mallard shot by participants of the NGC is approximately three times what it was in 1961.

What are flight ponds?

Flight ponds provide a feeding or roosting area for wildfowl. To feed the duck the keeper scatters barley or grain by hand on the water or at the edge of the pond to supplement natural food sources.

The creation of new flight ponds benefits a wide range of species. © GWCT

© *Laurie Campbell*

Mallard facts

Mallard are around 50-65 cm long, with the male being larger on average. Wing span is 81-98 cm. Very adaptable to an extremely wide range of habitats, breeding across the UK wherever there is a suitable wetland habitat – rivers, ponds or streams, standing or flowing fresh water, brackish estuaries or lagoons. Mallard generally prefer shallow water though, foraging only to a depth of around 1 metre and not choosing areas of deep water (more than a few metres) even for resting[32].

Mallard are mostly migratory. The UK hosts a breeding population of mallard, but also provides winter habitat for many that breed elsewhere. For example, many birds that breed in Iceland winter in Britain and Ireland.

A wide range of foods are eaten of both plant and animal origin. Mallard naturally feed on seeds, berries, plants insects and shellfish, but mallard are opportunistic and omnivorous. Food is usually obtained from or near the surface, although with occasional diving and the young do dive for food at 4-7 weeks. The mallard's diversity in feeding behaviour allows them to use a wide range of habitats[32].

Nest sites are variable, being mainly in cover – thick or thin, but occasionally in the open. Mallard readily use nest boxes or platforms, and nests can be fairly close together. The nests themselves are a shallow depression, with a low rim of grass, leaves or small twigs and lined with down.

Clutches of between 4 and 18 are possible, with an average of 13 in the UK. Replacement clutches tend to be slightly smaller, averaging 10. One egg is usually laid per day, which are then incubated for 27-28 days by the female, with the male sometimes nearby in the early stages[32].

The eggs are covered with down when the female leaves the nest. The young are mobile as soon as they hatch, and leave the nest on average 14-21 hours after hatching. They feed themselves straight away, but are cared for and brooded at night by the female, who protects them against predators. Ducklings fledge at 50-60 days, when they become independent[32].

Mallard rise straight off the water, leaping into the air and fly with shallow wing beats. Only the female makes the familiar deep quacking, while the male has a variety of calls. They live predominantly in flocks of various sizes which can consist of pairs or unpaired birds. Breeding in spring.

© Steven Watson

know?

You can make nesting tubes for mallard
Mallard will nest in tubes suspended on a pole on the water. These devices which are easy to make protect the brood from predation until they hatch.

Other duck species

In addition to mallard, eight other duck species are shot in the UK. Most are coastal and would be less likely to be found on an inland shoot: teal, wigeon, pintail, gadwall, shoveler, tufted, pochard and goldeneye. These are divided into two groups which align with their feeding strategies:

Dabbling ducks feed from the surface of water bodies, dipping their beaks to pick up food, or upending in shallow water. There are almost 40 separate dabbling duck species worldwide, including the quarry species mallard, pintail, gadwall, shoveler and teal. Wigeon are also dabbling ducks, but tend to feed by grazing for plants.

Teal are a dabbling duck, dipping their beaks into shallow water to feed.
© *Laurie Campbell*

Diving ducks as the name suggests, diving ducks dive under freshwater to find food. They also tend to have a slightly faster wingbeat than most dabblers. From the quarry species, tufted, pochard and golden-eye are diving ducks.

Geese

Native wild geese species on the quarry list comprise pink-footed, greylag, and white-fronted. Non-natives include Canada and Egyptian geese, both of which can currently be shot under certain general licences (see table 1).

© *Laurie Campbell*

What are the population trends for wildfowl quarry species?

Of the nine duck species on the quarry list, the breeding or wintering populations of eight have declined in recent decades. Two of the native goose species are suffering population declines. The area in which many of these species breed (the range) has also reduced. The reasons for this are not well established, and may be due to loss of wetland habitats, short-stopping of migrating wintering populations (see below) or other environmental changes.

There is no evidence that shooting is driving declines, indeed habitat management for wildfowl shooting may support the population as is seen for grey partridge. Studies examining this are lacking and it is important to adhere to responsible shooting practices to protect the populations of these winter visitors.

What is short-stopping?

Wildfowl are not wedded to using the same wintering grounds year on year, and simply follow their migratory routes until they reach a suitable area. Short-stopping is when ducks and geese stop earlier on their migration path, rather than travelling all the way to the destination, for example in the UK, that may have been used previously. It is though that short-stopping is occurring increasingly as a result of climate change, at least for some wildfowl species[140].

Basic wildfowl management

There has been a dramatic loss of wetland habitat over the past century, firstly because of land drainage, and more recently because of increased grassland management.

Partly because of their importance for breeding and nonbreeding wildfowl, three types of lowland wet grasslands that have declined substantially are included in the UK Biodiversity Action Plan (BAP) under three priority habitat types:

1. Coastal and Floodplain Grazing Marsh (UK Biodiversity Steering Group 1995)
2. Lowland Meadows (UK Biodiversity Steering Group 1995)
3. Purple Moor Grass and Rush Pastures (UK Biodiversity Steering Group 1998).

For example, there was a 40% reduction in coastal and floodplain grazing marsh between 1930 and the present day[141]. This has had a big impact on many species, but the reestablishment of such areas, often motivated by the prospect of improved shooting, can be hugely beneficial.

What habitat measures are performed for wildfowl?

There are three main techniques:

1. Reversion of pasture to bog or wetland
2. Pond creation and management
3. Reversion of arable land along the coast to wet grassland

How are these reversions achieved?

Where wet land has been converted to pasture or arable this will usually have been achieved with the addition of drainage. Blocking up the drains will allow the land to revert, becoming wetter and even flooding, which provides habitat for wildfowl.

What sort of pond management is done?

Sometimes ponds are created with a view to attracting or releasing ducks. When creating such a pond, the siting of it is important – often this is chosen by studying the existing behaviour of wildfowl in the local area. Being near a flight line is helpful.

Other important aspects are a range of depths, but mainly shallows; a rich variety of water plants, from marginal reeds and floating leaved forms to deeper submerged species; a number of islands or rafts; gently sloping shores, some of them open and mown, gravelled or grazed, and the whole surrounded by good tall meadow nesting cover and sheltered by a tree belt or hedge and stockproof fence.

Some plants will directly provide food through their leaves or seeds, some support other insects that are a food source, others provide shelter and may protect the banks from erosion. It is important to clear sufficient trees around the flight pond to let plenty of light in[142]. Increasing habitat availability and biodiversity with the creation of new ponds, or management for wildfowl of existing ponds, can be important for a wide range of other species.

Which predators are important?

Predation control may be necessary around wildfowl wetlands. As always, local variation will affect this, but in general foxes, crows and American mink are usually the biggest problem for predation on wildfowl. In some areas, the larger gulls can also predate ducklings. Predation control on wetlands can benefit a range of wading birds which like wildfowl are particularly vulnerable as ground nesters.

Old gravel pits

The GWCT has researched how good waterfowl habitat can successfully be created at the site of old gravel pits, and provide a new lease of life for such areas with many advantages for a range of other wildlife. The insight gained was relevant to wider wildfowl management. For example, early indications of poor productivity in mallard breeding around gravel pits led to detailed diet studies, which showed that ducklings need abundant invertebrates if they are to survive and grow. It soon became clear that food competition with fish was a key factor in this, so we now know that keeping ponds fish free makes a big difference in wildfowl conservation terms.

How was the gravel pit conversion achieved?

When gravel extraction is complete, groundwater will begin to fill the lakes naturally but this is not enough to provide good habitat. Ideally before the heavy machinery from quarrying leaves the site, pond landscaping should take place to optimise the layout of the lakebed and banks. Forming islands, sloping banks, shallow areas and reed beds at the start will lay the best foundations for suitable wildfowl and wildlife habitat[143]. The ability to control water flow via sluices to neighbouring water courses allows the raising or lowering of water levels to: flood meadows in winter, isolate nesting islands in spring/summer, fill scrapes and pools, expose wet mud feeding sites and other beneficial management activities[143]. In contrast, when left unmanaged, wet gravel pits can develop dense willow scrub at the edge, leading to low light penetration, low diversity and leaf litter clogging up the water.

There was a 40% reduction in coastal and floodplain grazing marsh between 1930 and 2018.

Ask the shoot

1. When do you commence shooting woodcock?

2. When do migratory woodcock arrive in the area?

3. What management are you doing for woodcock?

4. What's your local resident breeding population?

5. Have you created any wetlands on the shoot?

6. Do you release reared duck?

7. When are they released and when do you commence shooting them?

8. How do you ensure no there are no adverse impacts on the wild duck population or pond habitat?

9. Do you have sufficient alternative ponds for them to fly to once they have been driven?

© *Marie Gordon*

7. Lead ammunition

The use of lead as ammunition is an important, and topical, issue. There are many reasons for the historical and continued use of lead ammunition, as well as an important body of evidence looking at its impacts on human health, the environment and wildlife. The debate continues, and each individual will face a choice regarding their ammunition usage.

Developing alternatives is important for the ammunition industry, however there is still little information regarding the properties and potential effects of these.

Why do we use lead for ammunition?
Since the invention of firearms, lead has been used for bullets and shotgun pellets. Guns and rifles were designed with this ammunition in mind. Lead has properties that give the projectiles good range, penetration and lethality.

Is lead toxic to humans?

Yes. Along with some other common metals such as copper[144], aluminium and silver, lead is toxic[145]. There is no agreed safe level of lead[145].

What has been done to reduce exposure?

Increased knowledge about lead toxicity prompted the removal of lead from paint and petrol. This has reduced our lead exposure and blood lead levels are ten times lower than they were 30 years ago[146]. The main source of lead exposure now is from food[147].

Why is there lead in food?

Lead in found in soil, in very different amounts in different areas. This lead comes both from natural sources, for example the underlying bedrock, and from many different human sources such as industry and coal burning power stations contributing to lead in the atmosphere, which is then deposited in surface soils[146].

This can be taken up into plants destined to be food, or deposited onto them from the atmosphere. In general, the level of lead in the environment and our food is very low, and dropping in recent decades since the removal of some lead sources, but it does vary[147].

Which foods do we get the most lead from?

In the average diet, we ingest most of our lead through bread, tap water, beer, tea and potatoes. Although these foods contain very low levels of lead from background sources, they are consumed in relatively large quantities[147].

Who advises the government on food safety?

Human health toxicologists at the Food Standards Agency (FSA) and the European Food Safety Authority (EFSA). They both reported on lead in 2012[147,148].

What does the FSA think about eating lead-shot game?

FSA advice is that "frequent consumers of lead-shot game should eat less of this type of meat"[149], but has not given advice on the number of portions of lead-shot game that should be eaten because levels of lead in game are very variable.

Is this the same for everyone?

This advice is especially important for vulnerable groups such as toddlers and children, pregnant women, and women trying for a baby, as exposure to lead can harm the developing brain and nervous system[149].

Can I reduce my exposure by removing lead from the meat?

Careful butchering to remove lead shot and tissue from around the wound channel can help reduce, but does not eliminate lead exposure[150].

Can lead be dangerous to wildlife?

Yes. When waterfowl ingest spent shot mistaken for grit or foodstuffs it can result in lead poisoning. In addition, birds which are shot but not killed may carry lead shot in their muscles[151].

Is this why lead ammunition was banned over wetlands across Europe?

Yes. Legislation restricting the use of lead was introduced in England in 1999, Wales in 2002 and Scotland in 2004.

Has this legislation reduced wildlife deaths through lead poisoning?

We don't know. There have been no new studies of wildfowl lead ingestion since legislation was introduced. One estimate suggests that 73,000 wildfowl die each year in the UK, however this is still based on lead ingestion rates prior to the introduction of regulations banning lead ammunition for waterfowl[152].

Is there any evidence that lead is having a population-level impact on wildfowl?

Whilst there are negative impacts on individual birds exposed to lead, studies have not shown a direct effect of lead shot exposure on wild bird populations in the UK. There is evidence that exposure to lead shot may have a negative effect on mallard populations in France[151], and that lead from fishing weights affected mute swan populations in the UK[154]. These two sources of exposure have been removed for waterfowl by the wetlands lead shot restrictions, and the ban on lead fishing weights.

Lead ammunition: the law

The regulations regarding lead shot are not the same across the UK. In England and Wales, they are based on species as well as habitat, but in Scotland and Northern Ireland, lead use restrictions are only based on habitat.

In England and Wales the use of lead shot is prohibited as follows:

1. On or over any area below the high water mark.
2. On or over certain Sites of Special Scientific Interest. In addition, it is an offence to stand in a designated area and shoot a bird outside it with lead shot or to stand outside a designated area and fire lead shot over it.
3. For the shooting of ducks and geese of any species, coots or moorhens[153].

In Scotland and Northern Ireland, the use of lead shot is prohibited for shooting anything on or over all wetland areas. Wetland is defined under the Ramsar Convention, as areas of marsh, fen, peatland or water, whether natural or artificial, permanent or temporary, with water that is static or flowing, fresh brackish or salt; including area of marine water the depth of which at low tide does not exceed six metres. However, ducks and geese can be shot with lead over non-wetland areas in Scotland.

It is imperative that all who participate in shooting adhere to the legislation regarding the use of lead ammunition. Failure to do so not only risks the deposition of lead into sensitive habitats, but leaves both the individual and the shoot open to prosecution.

Is lead shot exposure is having an impact on gamebirds?

There is evidence that gamebirds can ingest shot into the gizzard when taking in grit, however this is seen at a lower level than in waterfowl. A GWCT study published in 2005 found that 4.5% of found dead birds contained shot in their gizzard, and estimated that 1.2% of living wild grey partridge contain ingested shot at any one time[155]. Other studies report similar findings in pheasants and red legged partridge, but do not record negative impacts on bird health[156,157]. One study in Canada demonstrated elevated lead levels in the liver of pheasants and some partridge species, without analysing the health consequences for those birds[158]. There is not enough evidence to know if lead shot exposure is having an effect.

What happens to lead shot in the muscles of birds?

Lead shot carried in living birds can gradually leach into the animal, and raise their exposure[156]. This may have impacts on the health and behaviour of the birds themselves, and some evidence suggests that birds exposed to sub-lethal levels of lead may be more susceptible to predation and other causes of death[159].

This also highlights another issue – if these birds are then predated, or die and are scavenged, the raised level of lead in their bodies and possible small fragments of lead shot may be consumed by predators or scavengers and pass up the food chain. Some studies find that birds of prey which eat gamebirds may have increased lead levels, and possibly lead poisoning, via this route[160]. A study on marsh harriers showed that they have higher blood lead levels, and more harrier pellets contain lead shot, during the hunting season than outside of it. It is thought that spent lead shot carried in the carcasses of prey is the source of this raised lead exposure[161].

Is there evidence of non-compliance with existing lead ammunition legislation?

Yes. Informal purchases of duck from game dealers in England show that up to 70% are still being shot illegally with lead[162], although the source of the duck was not known.

What non-lead ammunition is available?

Alternatives to lead ammunition are continually being developed using other metals including steel, copper, tungsten or bismuth.

Shot commonly referred to as "steel" is in fact manufactured from soft iron.

Do we know the environmental impacts of all these alternative ammunitions?

No. More research is needed. There is emerging evidence, for example, that tungsten may be carcinogenic[163,164], and possibly damaging to soil bacteria and earthworms at higher concentrations[165]. The impact of bismuth exposure is also an area which needs more investigation[166]. A thorough assessment of the alternatives is essential.

Are there other considerations around changing?

Because the ballistic properties of alternative ammunitions are different to lead, important parameters such as killing range will also differ. For example, the most common alternative, steel, is less dense and therefore does not carry as much energy as far as lead shot of the same size – meaning that there is more potential to wound rather than kill, if the reduced kill range is not remembered. When changing ammunition, remember that your shot size and shooting style may need to change.

Did you know? Informal purchases of duck from game dealers suggest that up to 70% are still being shot illegally with lead.

© Mike Short/GWCT

Follow the Code

Lead ammunition

"Shoot managers must ensure Guns comply with the relevant regulations restricting the use of lead shot"

"Guns must ensure they know and recognise the intended quarry species and comply with the relevant lead shot regulations"

"Guns should avoid depositing lead shot in wetlands important to feeding waterfowl"

The Lead Ammunition Group

Defra formed the Lead Ammunition Group in 2010 to review the science alongside other issues that needed to be taken into account, and make any recommendations both in relation to human health and wildlife. The terms of the group stated that a consensus should be reached by the group in the final report.

The group was chaired by John Swift (BASC Chief Executive until 2013) and included representatives from GWCT, the RSPB, Wildfowl & Wetlands Trust, Countryside Alliance, Gun Trade Association and the Game Dealers Association, as well as other professionals. On the government side, the Food Standards Agency and Defra were present.

The LAG spent many years researching this issue, and produced a comprehensive report in 2015. However, there was not agreement across the whole group as to the appropriate steps to be taken and some group members resigned.

The report and its supporting documents are available to read at: **www.leadammunitiongroup.org.uk/reports**

Ask the shoot

In England and Wales

1. Will there be a duck drive or evening flight?

2. Will there be a mixed game and duck drive?

3. If there is a SSSI – is it one where the use of lead shot on or over it is banned?

4. How do you ensure that the shoot and all Guns comply with the lead shot legislation?*

5. What do you do, in addition, to ensure no lead is dropped on wetlands?

In Scotland

6. Will we be shooting on or over any wetland?

7. How does the shoot ensure that Guns comply with the law on lead shot?

*It is important to make clear to the shoot that you will be keeping to the law and advise fellow Guns to do the same, if the shoot implies that using lead shot unlawfully does not matter.

© GWCT

8. Game as food

One of the Code of Good Shooting Practice's five golden rules is that game is food and must always be treated as such from the moment it is shot to the time it reaches the consumer. Failure to observe this rule demonstrates lack of respect for the quarry and brings shooting into disrepute. Guns have a responsibility to ensure any game shot is looked after and made good use of, whether it is being sold on or they are taking it home themselves.

Shoot managers should aim to produce fully mature, healthy and marketable game, a high percentage of which is fit for human consumption. No game should be shot within the withdrawal period for any medicines for which the birds have been treated (see chapter 9). It is unacceptable to shoot game that you know will not be fit for eating. On shoot day this begins with ensuring birds are picked up or collecting the birds as soon as possible. Birds should not be allowed to enter the food chain if they have been contaminated, for example, by landing in animal faeces.

The Code of Good Shooting Practice has prepared a Guide to Good Game Handling, which states that the basics of good handling of shot game includes keeping it clean, protecting it from contamination, rapid cooling and correct storage until it is processed. Regulations associated with the sale of game require it to undergo rapid cooling and that small game is stored at 4°C or lower. For most shoots that store game this will mean the need to use a suitable chiller.

Shot game should be kept clean, protected from contamination, cooled and correctly stored until it is processed for food preparation. © GWCT

Shoot participants such as Guns and pickers-up should put shot game in 'game carriers' which aid the cooling process, rather than closed bags. Good circulation of air helps cool game quickly, especially on warm early season days, so space birds out – lay them separately, and on their backs – never leave them in heaps as they will quickly begin to deteriorate. Any birds which are damaged or unfit for consumption should be kept separate from consumable game.

When game is being transferred to a suitable storage facility, a separate game cart or designated area within a vehicle should be used, again keeping space between the birds to encourage airflow between them. Shot birds should be taken to the game larder regularly throughout the day.

Any contaminated or otherwise unfit game should be kept separate and disposed of promptly within the law. Undiseased whole carcasses can be buried as long as it is done well away from any watercourse and beyond the reach of carnivorous animals. Any diseased game or part processed game (e.g. birds that have been breasted out) qualify as controlled waste and must either be incinerated in a Government-approved incinerator or rendered (pressure cooked) before going to landfill. Many shoots use a contractor for the disposal of birds properly deemed unfit for human consumption and the correct measn of disposal is essential so that actions such as burying are not misinterpreted as callous waste of good food.

The Code of Good Shooting Practice

GUIDE TO GOOD GAME HANDLING

Unless the game is being collected or delivered on the same day, the correct storage facility should be in place. The larder or chiller must be clean, fit for purpose, able to keep out flies and other contamination and be in good working order.

If game is not sold locally or to the end consumer it should go to a game dealer or an Approved Game Handling Establishment (AGHE). One of the legal requirements of an AGHE is that a trained person on the shoot has inspected the carcasses and holds Lantra's Level 2 Certificate in wild game meat hygiene or an equivalent. The one-day course is available through local colleges, and shows how to care for game destined to enter the human food chain. The Guide to Good Game Handling also strongly advises that those who supply game to third parties read the Wild Game Guide which explains the legal requirements in more detail. Find out more at **www.food.gov.uk/business-industry/farmingfood/wildgameguidance**

Follow the Code

Getting game into the foodchain
"Shoot managers must ensure they have appropriate arrangements in place for the sale or consumption of the anticipated bag in advance of all shoot days."

"Shoot managers should always offer Guns a brace of birds which Guns should accept. The practice of making oven-ready birds available is to be encouraged where practicable."

Did you know?

Game meat exports
Between 50-70% of British game meat is exported to Europe.

Ask the shoot

1. Before the shooting season, what provision do you have in place to sell your game?

2. Do you abide by the Guide to Good Game Handling?

3. Is your game sold to an Approved Game Handling Establishment?

4. Does someone on the shoot have Lantra's Level 2 Certificate in wild game meat hygiene or an equivalent?

5. Do you have a chiller?

6. Do you have a game cart?

7. What temperature do you keep your game?

8. Do you give Guns a brace at the end of the day and encourage them to take them?

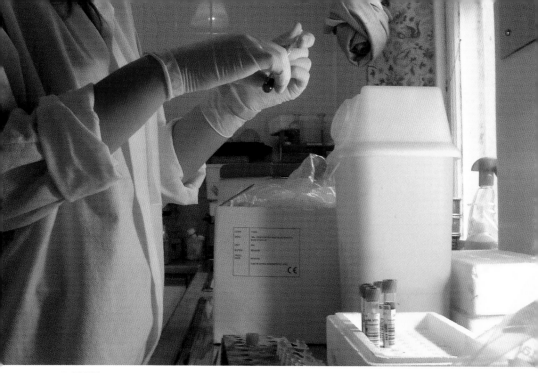

© GWCT

9. Diseases & Medication

Medication and Gamebirds

Modern game rearing, like other sectors of animal production, often requires use of medicines to ensure the health and welfare of gamebirds. All medicines used in game rearing must be prescribed and administered under the direction of a qualified vet.

Medicines that may be prescribed include antibiotics, wormers and anticoccidial products. The key to reducing the reliance on and the need for medications is to ensure there is very good husbandry and bio-security on the rearing field and in the release pens.

Antibiotic use in game birds

Antibiotics are an integral part of modern medicine and veterinary practice. However, bacteria which are resistant to antibiotics have been emerging, and this is a very real problem for the future. Reducing the use of those antibiotics we do have that are still working to as low a level as possible is seen as a global priority[167].

Are antibiotics used for game birds?

Yes. Antibiotics are used to treat sick gamebirds, as well as preventing the spread of disease outbreaks both where game are reared, and on shoots where they are released. The game industry is committed to playing its part in national and global antibiotic reduction, and it is imperative that everyone reviews their practice and reduce their usage as far as possible.

Are game farms and shoots responding?

Yes. The Game Farmers' Association (GFA) worked with the Veterinary Medicines Directorate so that measurements of the amount of antibiotics used in the game industry were recorded for the first time in 2016. This showed that three quarters of the active ingredient was given in feed, and a quarter in water[168]. Through improvements in practice, the amount of antibiotics used in the gamebird industry was reduced by more than a third in 2017. This progress is welcomed by the Veterinary Medicines Directorate, but it is important to continue reducing usage and hit the target of a further 25% reduction by 2020[169].

How are they reducing antibiotic use in gamebirds?

It is possible to reduce the need for antibiotics by improving biosecurity and game management. This makes it harder for disease to establish in the first place, and ensures conditions where, if disease occurs, it is less likely to thrive. Getting these things right can go a long way towards reducing the need for antibiotics.

At the game farm this means:
- a healthy parent flock
- clean disease-free eggs
- suitable stocking densities
- good quality food
- optimal conditions on the rearing field.

At the shoot, it is important to have:
- quality release pens with the right mix of habitats
- no standing water in and around release pens
- clean and plentiful drinking water
- good quality food.

Did you know?

The gamebird industry has been set the challenge of finding a further 25% reduction in antibiotic usage by 2020.

When should antibiotics be used for gamebirds?

"Antibiotics for incorporation into gamebird feed should not be prescribed at all unless the birds in question have been visited by the vet responsible for them or a clinical assessment of the birds has been undertaken by the vet (e.g. post mortem examination) <u>and</u> a need to prescribe has been established. Any departure from this general principle of responsible prescribing requires specific justification."

This means that antibiotics should only be given by the vet responsible for your birds, in the correct amounts, and in response to a need for them – not to prevent a need arising. There is also a compulsory 28-day withdrawal period between birds being treated with medication, before they can be shot, to ensure the meat is free of residue before it is eaten.

Justification to whom?

The enforcement body for this area is the Veterinary Medicines Directorate, who endorse the new best practice guidelines for prescribing antibiotics in gamebirds published in 2017. The following ten-point plan has already succeeded in reducing antibiotic use, but there is still a long way to go:

1. For the purposes of prescribing, all kept gamebirds must be "under the care" of a qualified veterinary surgeon. This means the vet has been given responsibility for the health of the flock by the owner. That vet must see the flock immediately before prescribing or have visited recently enough to make a diagnosis and prescribe.
2. Correct husbandry and management should always be in place and will reduce the need for medication and treatment.
3. Bird keepers must talk to their vet to establish whether there is a need to prescribe antibiotics before asking a feed company to compound rations containing medication.
4. Medicines prescribed under the 'cascade' system (which covers most of those used in gamebirds) can only be administered by a vet or someone directed by him or her and acting under his or her responsibility.
5. 'Cascade' medication is "in particular for the avoidance of unnecessary suffering".
6. Antibiotics must always be prescribed in response to a

specific need arising in the birds in question. They should never be used as a matter of habit or a substitute for good bird management.

7.   Where prescription of antibiotics is indicated, it must be for specific circumstances and for the exact amount necessary to resolve the problem.

8.   Owners should be advised on correct administration and storage of products, and appropriate withdrawal periods.

9.   Antibiotics must never be wasted or allowed to pollute the environment. Unused antibiotics must not be flushed to the sewer and should be disposed of as pharmaceutical waste.

10.   Any antibiotic use MUST be recorded.

These are available in full on the Game Farmers Association website at: **www.gfa.org.uk**

Ask the shoot

1.   What measures do you take to reduce the need for medication in your birds?

2.   Do you use foot baths outside your release pens?

3.   How often do you clean your drinkers?

4.   Do you move them?

5.   How often do you move your feed hoppers?

6.   Can you assure me that you stick to the 28-day withdrawal period for medicines?

GWCT scientists use radio-tracking to monitor tagged birds as part of their research © GWCT

10. Research & Monitoring

Research

What is now the Game and Wildlife Conservation Trust has a lengthy history, with perhaps surprising roots. The original ancestor of GWCT was the ICI Game Research Station in 1932, as a result of the forward thinking of Major H. G. Eley. At a time when little attention was paid to conservation for gamebirds, he realised that investment into cartridge technology to promote sales would be futile without similar efforts to protect the gamebirds themselves.

Practical research performed by gamekeepers and advisory officers at the first headquarters in Knebworth aimed to "make two birds fly where one flew before" through sensible conservation and game management. The underlying ideology of the trust of a sound basis in scientific research was established early when two scientists joined the Game Research Station in the first few years, and has remained a foundation of our work ever since. We now have over 60 scientists working at the GWCT.

Scientific research, the practical application of this knowledge and the much-needed advisory service have gone hand in hand throughout the history of the trust. The demand for education and training grew, and educational courses and keeper training followed to satisfy the need for high quality training on sustainable game and countryside management that meets best practice.

On a journey through changes of name and structure, the Game Research Station became the independent Game Conservancy in 1969, no longer associated with Eley Cartridges, and in 1980 became a charity – The Game Conservancy Trust.

GWCT runs a highly-valued training service to promote best practice. © GWCT

In order to better reflect the breadth of our work, the Game Conservancy Trust became the Game & Wildlife Conservation Trust in 2007. Today the GWCT is a pioneer in conservation research in areas both related and unrelated to game species and associated countryside management. Our approach allows the practical application of these techniques and contributes to sustainable increases in biodiversity across the countryside.

1. Our work is underpinned by robust scientific evidence.
Where this evidence exists, we work to apply it successfully. Where it is lacking, we address knowledge gaps with scientific research projects.

2. Application of scientific knowledge to the real world.

Using our demonstration sites and in collaboration with landowners, we test the application of scientific findings to demonstrate practicality. Examining the efficacy and practicality of techniques in this environment allows a genuine assessment of whether they will work when integrated into a farming or countryside management package.

3. Integration of practitioner feedback.

The input of practitioners who will apply and manage these conservation techniques on the ground is invaluable in assessing their viability.

4. Work to establish successful management techniques into policy.

When efficacy has been demonstrated, we work to integrate successful techniques into government policy, thus enabling inclusion in Agri-Environment Schemes, and incentive payments. This approach allows subsidies to be paid and therefore increases uptake by farmers, resulting in maximum benefit for wildlife.

5. Advisory service.

The GWCT runs an education and training service, to disseminate our knowledge of successful techniques, wherein we promote use of best practice in all aspects of countryside management.

6. Monitoring.

Long term monitoring projects allow evaluation of success and assessment of continual adjustments or improvements that can be made.

Our scientific reputation is based on the strength and quality of the research produced. Often researching areas that are not prioritised by others, we contribute to the understanding of game and wildlife, and improvements in biodiversity.

© GWCT

The GWCT developed from the ICI Game Research Station set up in 1932 to develop ways to protect wild game birds. ICI owned Eley cartridges at the time.

know?

On average, we produce 30-40 peer-reviewed papers in scientific journals each year, contributing to advancements in knowledge. Three particular areas of interest are: species recovery, how game management can contribute to wider biodiversity, and how land managers can do more alongside economic land use to improve wildlife conservation.

Scientific progress in all areas is driven by research, and this is no different in the field of game management. Our ongoing research programme continues to provide the evidence base for effective game management, conservation and environmental policy. We are still looking to improve outcomes for both game and biodiversity, and this book represents another effort to raise standards and strive for a working countryside that is rich in game and wildlife.

Insect sampling provides an insight into how land managers can do more to improve wildlife conservation alongside economic land use. © Jen Brewin

Long-term monitoring

The National Gamebag Census and Partridge Count Scheme

National long-term monitoring schemes can be seen as an early warning system for how species are faring, as well as helping us to understand recent changes in relation to historical ones. Understanding how numbers change over time is critical for managing wildlife populations, and long-term monitoring programmes underpin all effective wildlife management. Locally, they can help identify which management measures are helpful or damaging for different species, guide research into factors responsible for change, and inform management decisions on when and how to shoot quarry species.

How is it done?

By counting animals on an annual basis using consistent methods. There are lots of different national monitoring schemes in place, run by different organisations, covering for instance breeding bird abundance (British Trust for Ornithology, Royal Society for the Protection of Birds, Wildfowl & Wetlands Trust), mammal abundance (British Trust for Ornithology, Bat Conservation Trust, British Deer Society, Vincent Wildlife Trust, People's Trust for Endangered Species) and butterflies (Butterfly Conservation Trust). In order to monitor game and pest species, the GWCT runs two long-term monitoring schemes, the National Gamebag Census and the Partridge Count Scheme.

The GWCT National Gamebag Census (NGC)

What is the NGC?

The NGC is a voluntary nationwide system of bag monitoring, set up in 1961, formalising earlier surveys of game shooting begun at Oxford University in the 1930s (a "bag" is the number of a particular species that has been shot). At the end of each season, participating shoots submit their bag records to the GWCT's NGC Co-ordinator, who is responsible for maintaining the NGC database. More information on the NGC is available on the GWCT website, at: **www.gwct.org.uk/ngc**

What species are recorded in the NGC?

The NGC covers all quarry species and most so-called "pest" species that may be legally shot or trapped within the UK. The species covered include 25 huntable bird species, 12 "pest" bird species (species that may be killed or taken under General Licence) and 20 mammal species (see table 1).

Does that tell us how many are shot across the country?

No, because we do not know the percentage of shoots nationally that submit bag records to the NGC. But we can monitor national trends in bags of the different species by averaging changes in bag per unit area from year to year. The trends are relative to the start year, which is set to 1 and usually corresponds to 1961, when the NGC formally began.

Is it just how many are shot?

No, NGC participants also provide information on the number of shoot days, gamebird releases and bag composition. This is how the numbers shot were made up, for example in terms of young or old birds, female or male deer.

Why is this important?

The NGC is the only central UK database of bags from shoots and shooting estates. Because we have such long sets of reliable data, the bag records are an important source of information on long-term trends, in some cases reaching back over 100 years[170]. Changes in the number killed can give indications of changes in the underlying species abundance. For some species, in particular mammals, the NGC is the sole UK monitoring scheme able to provide trends over time[171]. They also give a unique historical perspective on changes in shooting itself[59]. More information on the mammals recorded in the NGC is available at: **www.gwct.org.uk/ngcmammals**

How do shoots take part and what does it cost to do so?

New contributors are always welcome, and we are most grateful to owners, keepers and shoot managers who send their returns to the NGC each season. Participation in the NGC is free, and there is no requirement to be a GWCT member. Individual shoot returns are kept strictly confidential, and the records contribute to an invaluable source of monitoring.

Did you know?

The National Gamebag Census, which relies on shoots volunteering information allows scientists to monitor trends dating back over 100 years.

As well as an annual census form, participants receive an annual newsletter that reviews bag trends of selected species and illustrates how NGC data can contribute factual information on topical issues.

Please sign up, or encourage your shoot providers to sign up, by visiting: **www.gwct.org.uk/ngc** or contacting the NGC co-ordinator at **ngc@gwct.org.uk**.

Huntable bird species	Pest bird species	Mammal species
Pheasant	Woodpigeon	Rabbit
Red-legged partridge	Feral pigeon	Brown hare
Grey partridge	Collared dove	Mountain hare
Red grouse	Carrion crow	Grey squirrel
Ptarmigan	Hooded crow	Brown rat
Black grouse	Magpie	Red deer
Common snipe	Rook	Sika deer
Jack snipe (NI)	Jackdaw	Fallow deer
Woodcock	Jay	Roe deer
Golden plover	Herring gull	Muntjac
Mallard	Great black-backed gull	Chinese water deer
Teal	Lesser black-backed gull	Wild boar
Wigeon		Hedgehog
Tufted duck		Fox
Pochard		Wildcat
Goldeneye		Feral cat
Pintail		Stoat
Shoveler		Weasel
Gadwall		Polecat
Pink-footed goose		American mink
White-fronted goose		
Greylag goose		
Canada goose		
Coot		
Moorhen		

Table 1. The NGC collects data on the following species.
NI: Northern Ireland

The Partridge Count Scheme provides feedback for participants about what management techniques are working well © GWCT

The GWCT Partridge Count Scheme (PCS)

What is the PCS?

The PCS is a voluntary scheme run by the GWCT and its predecessor organisations since 1933, to collect information on the annual abundance and breeding success of grey and red-legged partridges.

Can't this information come from the NGC?

No, the NGC records information about animals that are killed. The PCS collects count data on the number of partridges that are alive in spring and autumn. Many sites that contribute partridge counts to the PCS do not shoot, so would not participate in the NGC.

Why do we monitor partridges so closely?

Because grey partridges in particular are in need of conservation[172] (see chapter 3). We use the information from counts to estimate partridge breeding success and survival. If either or both of these values are low, they will prevent the population recovering. Using the counts, we provide feedback to participants about what management is working well and what additional management would help to address bottlenecks in the partridge life cycle. This further encourages landowners and managers to strengthen their efforts. This approach seems to work, as our research shows that PCS participants select more agri-environment options that benefit farmland birds than non-PCS participants[70].

What does it measure?

We encourage PCS participants to count their partridges twice a year, in spring, and in autumn after harvest:

- The spring count measures breeding abundance. How many are breeding?
- The autumn count measures breeding success. How well did they reproduce?

Counts are done in early morning and late evening when partridges are most active. Partridge counts are done using a four-wheel drive vehicle, which acts as a mobile 'hide' allowing large areas to be counted more easily. We provide participants with detailed instructions on how to count.

Who takes part?

Farmers, landowners, land managers, keepers, wardens, rangers – anyone who is interested in helping conserve grey partridges on their land, regardless of whether they shoot or not. We receive counts from wildlife trusts, the RSPB and National Nature Reserves as well as from farms and shoots.

How many grey partridges do you need in order to take part in the PCS?

There is no lower limit, nor do you have to be interested in them as a quarry species – every one counts. In fact, many participants do return 'zero' counts as it is also important for us to gather information from areas where there are few or no grey partridges.

© David Mason

know?

The Partridge Count Scheme contains many sites that do not shoot including RSPB-managed reserves and national nature reserves.

Taking part in the Partridge Count Scheme is a great way to understand how your management helping local partridge numbers. © Jen Brewin

How may I take part and what does it cost to do so?

New participants are always welcome, and we are ever grateful to participants who take the time to count their partridges and send us the results. Participating in the PCS is free, and individual returns are kept strictly confidential. Please sign up online at **www.gwct.org.uk/pcs**.

You do not have to be interested in shooting grey partridges or be a GWCT member to take part, it is grey partridge conservation that is paramount. PCS participants receive instructions on how to count partridges, are sent spring and autumn newsletters and invitations to grey partridge meetings and farm walks. Based on returned counts, they receive help and advice on how to improve the environment for grey partridges and how to provide the additional support the birds may need[69].

Ask the shoot

1. Are you a member of the National Gamebag Census?

2. Are you a member of the Partridge Count Scheme?

© *GWCT*

11. What Guns need to know on a shoot day

Though not within GWCT's scientific remit, we believe it would be wrong to produce a guidebook for responsible Guns without including certain elements of safety, good conduct and the law relating to a day's driven game shooting.

We have excluded much relating to shoot day etiquette, or appropriate dress as there are plenty of comprehensive guides on these areas already published. The text below is largely taken from *Sporting Shooting and the Law* published by the National Gamekeepers' Organisation with kind permission of the author David Frost and the NGO. There is much further content relating to certification, rifle shooting and other legal matters contained in the booklet, which is recommended reading and available through the GWCT online shop.

Driven vs rough shooting

Most let days shooting are driven days but you may also be invited on or have the opportunity to take a rough shooting day. The guidelines outlined in this chapter apply equally to both, but there are differences in the form of the day.

Rough shooting

A rough shooting day is when a group of Guns walk with dogs to flush birds along hedges, or through woods, fields or game cover. It may take place on a larger shoot as a boundary day round the edges of the main shoot, or be part of a rough shooting syndicate.

The latter would release far fewer birds than a driven shoot and either own the land or rent the shooting rights from local farmers or estates. There is no reason why these syndicates shouldn't undertake the conservation work described in the preceding chapters on a voluntary basis, but they would be less likely to be able to afford to employ a gamekeeper.

Driven shooting

Driven shooting developed in the mid-to-late 1800s. Rather than walking up the birds, Guns stand while the birds are driven over them by beaters. They can be wild birds if numbers are sufficient but are normally reared. There are various arrangements for driven shoots, which would usually employ a gamekeeper.

The shoots might be paid for and managed solely for the landowners' personal recreation, or some days may be let to visiting Guns to help pay for the gamekeeper's salary and other costs. Another model is for the landowner to lease the shooting rights to a syndicate of Guns who take on the running of the shoot themselves.

Alternatively, a sporting agency, individual, or company may buy or lease the shooting rights and take on the responsibility for running and financing the shoot and sell days to outside Guns or syndicates. Whatever the shoot's management structure, all shoots should undertake the conservation measures described in the previous chapters and must abide by both the numerous regulations governing shoot operations and the Code of Good Shooting Practice.

On a driven day beaters flush the game from cover. It is vital to be aware of their position at all times.
© GWCT

Beaters, stops and pickers-up

On a driven shoot, beaters flush the birds over the Guns by walking in a line through the woods or game cover crops. Some beaters take on the role of stops who are placed to prevent game breaking out of the side of the drive. The pickers-up wait behind the Guns during the drive ready to collect the game with their gundogs as soon as the drive is over. To stay safe, it is vital to be aware of those around you at all times. Though the beaters and pickers-up get paid by the shoot, it is a token amount. They are likely to live locally and for them it is as much a social event and a chance to get out into the countryside and work their dogs. It is important to treat them with courtesy and thank them as well as the keeper at the end of the day. A shoot day is a team effort led by the gamekeeper and including beaters, pickers-up and Guns and everyone should work together to make sure best practice is observed.

Follow the Code

Shooting associations
"Seek to help and support the relevant associations that represent and promote your sport"

Health and safety

Before you take up shooting

Observance of the safety rules is an integral part of good gun ownership. Newcomers to gun ownership are advised to visit a reputable shooting school for a series of lessons to ensure they can handle a gun safely and proficiently before starting shooting. In the UK, we are fortunate to have a wide range of weekly and monthly shooting periodicals containing news and articles of interest both to the newcomer and the experienced sportsman.

They are well worth reading to keep up to date with developments in the shooting world. You should also join a relevant organisation such as GWCT, BASC, the Countryside Aliiance, and the National Gamekeepers Organisation. Membership gives access to a wide range of services and ensures long term support for you and your sport.

Insurance

Although not a legal requirement in the UK it is strongly recommended that you never shoot unless you are adequately insured for injury and damage to third parties. It also makes sense to insure your own guns and shooting equipment against damage or loss. All the major shooting organisations offer insurance cover. Check the terms carefully as some activities, such as beating, loading and picking up, may not be covered if you are paid to do them.

Basic gun safety rules

a)   Never load your gun except when you are about to use it. Unload it immediately after use.
b)   Never point a gun at anyone, whether it is loaded or not.
c)   Keep your guns and ammunition away from children and other unauthorised persons at all times.
d)   Check that your gun is unloaded on every occasion on which you pick it up.
e)   When handing a gun to someone else open the breech (or equivalent) and show it is unloaded before passing it over.
f)   Never load a gun indoors.
g)   Check that the barrels are not damaged or obstructed before loading.

h)   Never shoot unless you can see it is safe to do so. Except when shooting ground game it is a sound principle to be able to see sky below the barrels when the trigger is pulled.

i)   Never shoot at game which is near to a Gun, picker up or beater.

j)   Never swing through the line.

k)   Remain calm and steady throughout.

Check your gun is empty on every occasion you pick it up © GWCT

The safety catch

The safety catch is often not what it seems. Safety catches work in several different ways and you should familiarise yourself with the one fitted to your gun. Ideally the catch should lock the firing pin and the triggers but in most shotguns and in some other guns it only locks the triggers.

This means that if the gun is defective it could fire when the safety catch is on. Although most shotguns have automatic safety catches there are some which do not, so check before using a borrowed gun. You should never place too much reliance in the safety catch as a means of preventing accidental discharge although it should always be on except when you are about to fire.

A shoot employing five or more people has to have a health and safety policy

If your shoot employs five or more persons such as keepers, paid beaters or pickers up, even on a casual or temporary basis, you are required to have a written safety policy and bring it to the attention of your employees. A good time to do this is at the pre-shoot briefing. Because of the risk of noise damage to hearing you should ensure that hearing protectors are made available to any employee likely to be close to a gun when it is fired.

Employees must be properly trained in the use of any equipment or chemicals used in connection with shoot management or game rearing. Health and safety is often regarded by shoots as a tedious distraction but it does need to be taken seriously. The NGO website has excellent guidance on health and safety policy and risk assessments.

Shoot captain's briefing

The shoot captain, host or manager should brief all Guns and other shoot participants, however experienced, at the start of each day's shooting. The brief should always include a reminder about the importance of gun safety, as well as any local rules about the shooting of pests, game and ground game. Guns, beaters and pickers up will have a more enjoyable day if they know what is planned to take place. Especially on a new shoot, do not be afraid to ask questions at the briefing if there is anything about which you are uncertain.

When walking it is best to carry the gun in the crook of the arm, broken, with the barrels pointing forward and down. © GWCT

Carrying a gun safely

a)   In a vehicle and when walking into position unload the gun and put it in a slip or case.

b)   When walking it is best to carry the gun in the crook of the arm, broken, with the barrels pointing forward and down.

c)   The alternative is to carry it over your shoulder with the triggers uppermost and the barrel pointing in the air. This is not recommended on hilly land because of the risk that you may find the gun pointing at somebody higher up the hill, or that in the event of a fall the barrels could end up pointing at somebody.

d)   If your gun is fitted with a sling carry it over one shoulder with the muzzle pointing vertically in the air.

e)   Except during walked up shooting, never walk with the gun in the "ready" position i.e. with one hand on the barrel and the other near the triggers. Even then it should be pointing at the ground.

f)   Between drives the gun must be unloaded. It is normal for guns to be broken or carried in a slip.

g)   In thick cover or on rough ground, walk with the gun unloaded, even if it may mean missing a shot.

h)   Unload your gun before crossing a fence or other obstacle.

Dangers of mixing ammunition

Never keep cartridges of different bores together. A 20-bore cartridge accidentally loaded into a 12-bore gun (or 28 bore into 16 bore) will jam in the barrel beyond the chamber. A 12-bore cartridge can then be loaded inadvertently and fired. This almost invariably bursts the barrel and causes serious injury.

There are also several rifle cartridges which can be dropped into or even fired in the wrong chamber with possibly disastrous effects. Before shooting, check that the bore is clear and that the ammunition in your pocket is designed for the chamber of your gun. This requires an understanding of ballistics including gauge, shot size, load, pattern and choke for both steel and lead shot.

Quarry, predator and pest species

Definition of Game – England and Wales

Strangely, there is no single legal definition of game and its meaning varies from act to act. The term always includes pheasants, partridges, grouse and black game. The archaic term moor and heath game is sometimes used. In some legislation game also includes hares, rabbits, bustard, woodcock, snipe and ptarmigan. Deer are never mentioned in the game acts but have protection under their own legislation. Dictionaries define game as wild animals and birds hunted for food and sport. This wider definition includes deer and wildfowl.

Deer are mentioned in the Game Acts but have their own legislation.
© *Peter Thompson*

Definition of game – Scotland

The concept of game no longer exists under Scottish law. Birds and animals that were previously considered to be game are now classed as wild birds and animals. They are now subject to the provisions of the Wildlife and Countryside Act which, with some exceptions, makes it an offence to be in possession of any wild bird or its egg.

However, mallard, pheasants, partridges and grouse which are being reared for release are not regarded as wild animals until they are released so the traditional breeding and release of gamebirds is not affected.

Vermin

There is no legal definition of vermin for the purposes of the Firearms Act. It is generally taken to include any species which causes damage to crops, wildlife or property including rabbit, mink, stoat, weasel, brown rat, grey squirrel, woodpigeon, magpie, rook and crow. Although vermin is the term used in certificates, the terms pest and predator are often preferred and have the same meaning for most practical purposes.

Shooting game at night, on Sundays and on Christmas day

Game, as defined in the Game Act 1831, means all the species listed in Part 1 of Appendix A. These may not be shot at night (i.e. from one hour after sunset to one hour before sunrise). In England and Wales it is illegal to shoot these species on Sundays and on Christmas day. No such restriction applies in Scotland but it is customary not to shoot game on these days.

Limits on shooting wildfowl and certain other birds

The birds listed in Parts 3 and 4 of Apendix A may not be shot on Sundays or Christmas Day in Scotland. Nor may they be shot on Sundays in the former counties and county boroughs of Anglesey, Brecknock, Caernarvon, Cardigan, Carmarthen, Cornwall, Denbigh, Devon, Doncaster, Glamorgan, Great Yarmouth, Isle of Ely, Leeds, Merioneth, Norfolk, Pembroke, Somerset and the North and West Ridings of Yorkshire. The prohibition also extends to shooting ducks and geese under general licence. The boundaries apply to these areas as they existed before local government reorganisation in 1974.

General licences to control pest species

Certain species of birds which are regarded as pests are technically protected under EU legislation and the Wildlife and Countryside Act and may only be taken or killed by authorised persons under the authority of a general licence. Part 5 of Appendix A lists the species to which this applies. The licences, of which there are several, are renewed annually, usually on 1 January, by Natural England, Scottish Natural Heritage and the Welsh Assembly Government.

It is legal to shoot wildfowl on Sundays in certain counties of England and Wales.

The terms of the licences often differ between the three jurisdictions. You do not need to have a copy of the licence yourself, but you must have the oral or written authority of the owner or occupier before you go shooting or trapping. Most licences authorise the use of a semi-automatic shotgun. The terms of the licences are specific and are typically limited to conserving wild birds, protecting any collection of wild birds, preserving public health or public or air safety, preventing the spread of disease or preventing serious damage to livestock, foodstuffs for livestock, crops, vegetables, fruit, growing timber or fisheries. In 2015 two potential alien invasive species, not then found in the UK, were added to the English list so as to pre-empt them becoming established.

Before shooting or trapping one of the listed species you must satisfy yourself that you are doing so for one of the permitted reasons. Shooting for sport is not acceptable under any general licence. In all cases you are required to satisfy yourself that non-lethal methods of control are ineffective or impractical but you do not need to have tried other methods before using a trap or gun. The judgement is a purely personal one based on your own experience of shooting and pest control.

You can view the licences on the various websites and it is essential that you do so before your first outing each year. It is important for the ongoing future of the licensing system that anyone controlling pest or predator species does so strictly in accordance with the terms of the licences.

Did you know?

Two alien species not then found in the UK were added to the English general licences to pre-empt them from becoming established.

© *Francesco Veronesi*

© GWCT

Range and distance

Estimating range

Guns must be competent at estimating range, and shoot within the limitations of their equipment to kill cleanly and consistently. This requires an understanding of ballistics including gauge, shot size, load, pattern and choke for both steel and lead shot. For a comprehensive theoretical explanation of ballistics see *The BASC Handbook of Shooting*. Training at a shooting school before shooting live quarry is advised.

A good Gun knows their limitations

As well as an understanding of ballistics, making a clean kill is dependent on the Gun's ability. The shoot management team has a duty to tailor drives to your level and Guns should leave birds, if they are not shooting adequately.

High birds

Having developed an understanding of range, Guns have a responsibility not shoot at excessively high or out-of-range birds. Equally, shooting low or close-range birds is unsafe and may render them unfit for human consumption.

Don't forget to pick up your empties

Guns should always use degradable wads where possible and all cartridges cases and litter should be removed after each shoot.

Retrieval and handling of game

Gundogs

Before embarking on any form of live quarry shooting, Guns must ensure that adequate provision has been made for the retrieval of the game they shoot and shooting should not be conducted where it is not possible to retrieve shot game. This means Guns must own or have access to a trained gundog on the day.

Guns must ensure that adequate provision has been made for picking up. © A.Hook

Pickers-up

On a driven day, shoot managers must ensure that adequate provision is made to retrieve game as soon as it is shot. Making sure there is a big enough team of pickers-up is an essential part of this process. The larger the bag the greater number of pickers-up required.

Marking birds

Guns have a responsibility to mark the fall and assist in the retrieval of every bird they shoot. This includes checking with pickers-up that all their birds have been collected and helping them where practical to do so. Guns should also help in the retrieval of game shot by others.

Humane despatch

Guns and pickers-up must ensure that they despatch any wounded quarry without delay and in a humane manner. Never shoot wounded game as it is dangerous and may render it useless for eating. A sharp knock on the back of the head with a stick or priest is the best method.

Dogs are an essential part of helping shoot managers to ensure that adequate provision is made to retrieve all shot game. © GWCT

Follow the Code

Picking-up during the drive
"On driven days, any wounded game should be retrieved during drives whenever it is safe and practicable to do so"

Adequate provision for retrieval of game
"Shoot managers must ensure that adequate provision is made to retrieve all shot game and dogs are an essential part of this process"

Practice on clay targets
"Inexperienced Guns should improve personal shooting skills through practice on clay targets and must be accompanied and supervised by a suitably experienced person."

Leaving enough time for pickers-up to do their job
"A day's game shooting should finish early enough to allow time for pickers-up to complete their task before the birds start to go to roost"

Respect for the quarry is paramount
"It is fundamental to mark and retrieve all shot game which is food and it must be treated in accordance with the Guide to Good Game Handling"

© GWCT

Shooting and the public

Bringing shooting into disrepute

Guns should remember that others will judge the shooting community by their behaviour and the actions of their fellow Guns. If you see others behaving in a way likely to bring the sport into disrepute, politely make them aware of their duty to the shooting community as a whole.

Codes of conduct

First and foremost use courtesy and politeness with the public at all times. Make sure you are aware of any public rights of way and avoid frightening, obstructing or endangering users. Shooting or beating should be paused to allow horses or walkers to pass. Avoid shooting birds over another's property or shooting near other properties, if it may be a nuisance.

Be aware that:
- Shooting across any right of way may constitute a wilful obstruction or public nuisance, which is a criminal offence.
- It is a civil offence to allow shot to travel over a boundary on to another property
- It is an offence to be drunk in possession of a loaded gun

> **Follow the Code**
>
> **Shooting is judged by how you behave**
>
> *"Shooting and shoot management practices will be judged by the way participants and providers behave"*

Carrying a shotgun in a public place/staying away from home

You may not carry a loaded shotgun in a **public place** without lawful authority or reasonable excuse. The onus of proving lawful authority or reasonable excuse lies with the person carrying the gun. Reasonable excuse could include, when out shooting, having a loaded shotgun on a footpath running across the shoot. The police have the power to examine guns if they have reason to believe this part of the law is being infringed.

It is bad practice to shoot near a public footpath. © GWCT

Public place

Broadly speaking a public place is anywhere to which the public have, or are permitted to have, access (by payment or otherwise) and includes public footpaths and public highways. Thus some parts of a shoot may be a public place whilst others are not. Vehicles are considered to be in a public place whilst they are on the highway. Open access legislation, especially in Scotland, has turned large areas of open land into a public place.

Shooting near roads/rights of way

There is a common misconception that all shooting within fifty feet of the highway is prohibited – it is not. In England and Wales it is an offence to discharge a firearm within fifty feet of the centre of a highway if in consequence a user of the highway is injured, interrupted or endangered. For this purpose a highway is any road over which the public have a right of way in a vehicle.

A footpath, cycle way or bridle path is not a highway but it is good practice not to shoot close to a path which is being used by the public. You are not allowed to shoot if you are standing on a public road or its verge. It is widely accepted in Scotland that you are not precluded from shooting from a public highway, but reckless discharge would apply under common law if you were to inconvenience or disturb others using the highway.

Follow the Code

Positioning of release pens
"Release pens where possible should be sited out of public view"

Roadkill pheasants
"Game managers should collect and dispose of road casualties where possible"

Released pheasants in neighbours' gardens
"Released birds should be managed to avoid damage to neighbouring crops or gardens"

Frequency of shooting
"The frequency of shooting must not give rise to unreasonable nuisance (particularly noise) to neighbours"

Certification and permission

Production of certificates

The police have powers to demand the production of shotgun certificates from people they believe to be in possession of shotguns or ammunition, and to seize the guns in the event of noncompliance. For this reason you should always take your certificate with you when out shooting. However, modern technology should make this unnecessary as the police can easily check, even out of working hours, whether you are a genuine certificate holder.

Certificates contain a large amount of personal information. In order to reduce the risk of identity fraud if the certificate is stolen from your car you may find it easier to carry a photocopy with the address, date of birth and signature blanked out. Some police forces try to insist that you send in the expiring certificate when you apply for a new one. There is no legal authority for this and you lay yourself open to having your guns confiscated if you are found in possession and unable to produce a certificate at the time. Offer the police a scan or photocopy of the certificate if they wish to check it against their records.

Age limits

There is no minimum age at which a person may be lent a shotgun and hence no minimum age for obtaining a shotgun certificate. The age limits for possessing shotguns are:

> Anyone under the age of 15 who has an assembled shotgun with him must be under the supervision of a person aged at least 21 unless the gun is in a securely fastened gun cover such that it cannot be fired. There is no legal definition of "supervision" in this context but common sense dictates that the supervisor should be close enough to the user to ensure he can control the actions of the person he is supervising. It is recommended that, except during properly organised target shooting, supervision should be on a one to one basis. In some cases it is cheaper and more convenient for an adult to keep a shotgun intended for use by a young person on his own certificate and then loan it rather than for the youngster to apply for a separate certificate. Persons under the age of 15 may not buy or be given a shotgun but they may be lent one.

- **15 to 17** - You may be given a shotgun but you cannot buy a gun or ammunition. You may shoot unsupervised.
- **18** - This is the minimum age at which you may purchase or hire a shotgun and ammunition.

Borrowing a shotgun

Anyone may borrow a shotgun from another person on **private premises** provided certain conditions are met

a.   The lender must be aged 18 or over and must hold a certificate in respect of the gun being loaned.

b.   The shotgun may only be used for shooting game or vermin or shooting at artificial targets. Game in this context means animals and birds hunted for food or sport, so includes wildfowl. Artificial targets include clays.

c.   The lender must be either
   i.   A person who has the right to allow others to enter the premises for the purposes of shooting game or vermin. Game in this context includes wildfowl.
   ii.   A person who is authorised in writing by a person in c(i) above to lend the shotgun either generally or to specific individuals.

d.   The borrower must comply with the conditions in the lender's certificate.

e.   The borrower must be in the presence of the lender or of another person **authorised** under c(i) or c(ii) above who holds a shotgun certificate.

Private premises

Private premises means premises to which the public have no access other than by permission of the owner, **occupier**, or lessee of the premises. Premises includes both buildings and land.

Authorised person

An authorised person for most purposes is the owner or occupier of the relevant land or any person authorised by the owner or **occupier**, including the shooting tenant and gamekeepers. In some cases, local authorities and certain statutory authorities may also grant authority.

Occupier

Under the Wildlife and Countryside Act 1981 an occupier, in relation to any land other than the foreshore, includes any person having any right of hunting, shooting, fishing or taking game or fish.

Presence and supervision

The word "presence" appears several times in the Act and is generally understood to mean within sight and/or earshot, although there is no clear legal definition. In a 2011 Crown Court case in Mold it was held that someone shooting rabbits with a borrowed rifle from an upstairs window was in the presence of the certificate holder who was in a downstairs room. "Supervision", also found in the Act in relation to young persons, requires that a tighter level of control be exercised over the user.

Casual use

A shotgun certificate may be issued even though the applicant has no intention of acquiring a gun of his own. This might be the case, for example, where the applicant wishes to borrow a shotgun for periods of 72 hours or less but not be subject to the restrictions placed on borrowed shotguns.

Carrying a gun for another person

Under Section 11(1) of the Act no certificate is needed if you are carrying a shotgun or ammunition belonging to someone else for use by that person for sporting purposes. This exemption is mainly intended to cover loaders on a shoot day and does not permit unaccompanied transport of the guns concerned, such as by a chauffeur. If the bearer is under 18 the person for whom the gun is being carried must be over 18.

Retrieving shot game from neighbouring land

In England and Wales you commit trespass if you shoot game or pests over your own land which falls alive or dead on your neighbour's ground and either you or your dog goes to fetch it. Despite the obvious animal welfare considerations there is no automatic right to retrieve wounded birds or animals from neighbouring land. Shoots and private individuals should come to a reciprocal arrangement which allows for wounded birds to be retrieved. Failing such an arrangement, the wounded creature will have to be left.

Trespass

Anyone who enters, shoots on or sends his dog on land without the permission of the landowner, or in contravention of open access legislation, is a trespasser and may be sued for damages or in persistent cases be restrained by injunction or interdict. Trespassers may be asked to leave the land and be escorted to the boundary using no more force than is necessary. It is also trespass to exercise lawful rights in such a way as to interfere with the land over which the rights are exercised. So, for example, people who walk repeatedly along a public footpath in such a way as to disrupt a shoot might be restrained by an injunction or be subject to a claim for damages.

Armed trespass – England and Wales

If you are carrying a firearm, shotgun, antique firearm or air gun, whether loaded or not and even if you have no ammunition, it is an offence to trespass without reasonable excuse. Reasonable excuse is not clearly defined so if for any reason you need to enter into land over which you do not have the shooting rights or other right of access you should leave your gun behind. Whereas trespass is a matter for civil action, armed trespass is a criminal offence.

Armed trespass – Scotland

In Scotland the Land Reform Act (Scotland) 2003 and the accompanying Scottish Outdoor Access Code have effectively modified the provisions of the Firearms Act in relation to armed trespass. In Scotland you would not be guilty of armed trespass if you were crossing land or water to get directly to or return directly from other land or water over which you had the right to shoot. If you were on land or water or in a building for any other purpose the offence of armed trespass would still be committed.

Sporting rights - England and Wales

In England and Wales the right to kill wild animals and birds lies with the occupier of the land unless the landowner has specifically reserved this right for himself. The holder of the sporting rights may exercise them himself, lease them or give oral permission to somebody else to exercise them. A shooting lease should always be in writing and by deed as oral permission only confers a licence to shoot,

PRIVATE PLEASE KEEP OUT

although if oral permission has been given and rent paid the tenant would be entitled to reasonable notice of termination. Ideally leases should be drawn up by a solicitor and use such wide ranging phrases as "hunting, shooting, killing and carrying away all manner of game, wildfowl and other wild animals and birds".

Shooting rights do not automatically include the right to rear and release game so this must be included if you wish to do so. The Country Land and Business Association and BASC have model sporting leases. In its legal sense the word "game" has a narrow meaning and if used alone could be unduly restrictive. Any game killed is the property of the holder of the sporting rights, as is any game shot over the land but which falls on neighbouring land.

Shooting over a boundary constitutes poaching © A.Hook

Sporting rights - Scotland

Scottish law differs slightly and the right to kill birds and animals lies with the landowner unless he has expressly let it to the tenant. The right to kill ground game lies with the occupier. If the tenant of the land also has the shooting rights he is not allowed to sublet without the permission of the landowner so it follows that the shooting tenant should normally hold his lease from the landowner.

Poaching – England and Wales

Anyone trespassing by entering on land in pursuit of game, woodcock, snipe or rabbits may be committing a poaching offence. Searching for game without actually having taken any is sufficient to count as poaching. Poaching at night is a more serious offence than poaching during the day, particularly if the poachers are numerous and armed with firearms or other weapons. Shooting over the boundary constitutes poaching irrespective of whether you or your dog retrieve the game. Taking or destroying the eggs of game also constitutes poaching. There is a little known power arising from Code B of the Police and Criminal Evidence Act 1984 which gives the police the right to require a person to retain an object as evidence. This can be useful for dealing with poachers especially if dogs etc are concerned. It means the owner cannot dispose of the item without risking prosecution and can potentially be hugely inconvenient to a suspected poacher.

Poaching – Scotland

The former legislation covering poaching has been repealed and the offence is now covered under revisions to the Wildlife and Countryside Act which gives the police greater powers than they had under the old legislation. It is an offence to take any bird (or its eggs) or animal without having the legal right to do so. Enforcement lies with the police and there are no special powers for landowners or gamekeepers. Searching for game without actually having taken any does not constitute poaching but can be prosecuted as an attempt to commit an offence under the Wildlife and Countryside Act.

Single witness evidence is admissible for certain offences involving grouse, partridge, pheasant and ptarmigan. If you shoot game over your own land and it falls alive on neighbouring land you would be a poacher if you or your dog went to retrieve it but you could always argue it was mercy killing.

Security

Guns in transit and on shoot days

The law is vague on what constitutes 'stored securely' and 'reasonably practical' when guns are being carried away from home. It is generally acceptable for guns to be left out of sight in a locked car for short periods (e.g. during lunch) but the car itself should be somewhere that you can see it.

Whilst a higher level of security might be appropriate if guns are regularly left unattended in a vehicle for long periods this would not apply to most sporting users. Never leave your guns unattended in an unlocked car, even for a few minutes – thieves can strike at the most inopportune moment. For overnight stops with friends or in hotels the gun should be locked in the most secure place available. Guns being carried in public should be in a slip or case. When a gun is left anywhere other than in its normal storage a key component such as the forend or bolt should be removed and kept on your person. Expect no sympathy if your gun is stolen intact. Pub car parks are popular venues for thieves and extra care should be taken if you are lunching in a pub.

Overnight storage in a hotel

Some hotels have a secure gun storage but check that the person with control of the storage is a shotgun certificate holder (if you are lodging a shotgun) or RFD (for rifles and/or shotguns), otherwise it would be unlawful to give the gun to them. Ensure you get a receipt. In some cases it may be best if the owner can keep the gun with him at all times or keep different parts of the gun in different places.

Please give us your feedback!

The GWCT believes that the information this book contains should be spread as widely as possible through the shooting community, and would encourage others to borrow from it and share this knowledge, provided of course acknowledgement is made. Equally, as part of this project we are keen to have reader feedback and suggestions for improvements. Please contact us at **info@gwct.org.uk**

Glossary

Agri-environment schemes
A government-funded mechanism aimed to support farmers and land managers in adopting techniques or management measures that are beneficial to the environment.

Ancient semi-natural woodlands:
Areas of woodland that have been continuously wooded since 1600 in England and Wales, and since 1750 in Scotland.

BASC
The British Association for Shooting and Conservation: *www.basc.org.uk*

Beetle bank
A raised earth bank constructed across the middle of large arable fields, sown with a mix of tussocky, perennial grasses, and disconnected from the existing field edges. This habitat provides ideal nesting cover for grey partridges, as well as overwintering sites for predatory, beneficial insects.

Beneficial insects
Beneficial insects are: pollinators, decomposers, chick-food insects and butterflies, as well as predatory insects that are the natural enemies of pest species, eating pests such as greenfly within crops and can therefore be beneficial to the farmer in controlling these.

Biodiversity Action Plan
A government program to identify and protect threatened species and habitats. The UK biodiversity action plan was published in 1994, as the UK's response to the Convention on Biological Diversity held in Rio de Janero in 1992, and which the UK signed up to. Species and habitat lists were published in 1995 and 1999, and reports are published every three to five years looking at how the BAP is contributing to the UK's progress towards reducing biodiversity loss.

Biodiversity assessment
The GWCT advisory service offers the shoot biodiversity assessment. They will thoroughly survey the shoot and the management methods in place, examine the game and wildlife and how it is managed, and give a confidential report with an action plan for future improvement for the shoot, and the biodiversity.

Brooding
A parent bird uses their wings or body to protect the chicks and keep them warm early in life when their own temperature regulation is not yet developed and they are most vulnerable to the cold and wet.

BTO
British Trust for Ornithology: *www.bto.org*

Conservation Headland
A strip around the perimeter of an arable field that is treated with no or few herbicides and insecticides, and are often drilled more widely than the main cropped area to increase the space between rows and allow chicks to move through it more easily. Conservation headlands are designed to provide insect-rich brood cover for the early weeks of life, when gamebird chicks need insect foods. They contain more arable weeds and wildflowers than the rest of the crop, provide chick food insects for game birds, and many benefits for other species.

Corvids
The crow family of birds, that includes the carrion crow, hooded crow, raven, magpie, jackdaw, rook and jay.

Covey
A group of partridge (or grouse) – usually a family group, but sometimes with additional lone adults, which stay together through the summer and winter, breaking up in January or February into pairs, whereupon there is some dispersal.

Exclosure
An area which is fenced off to protect from certain species, for example predators, by keeping them out.

Exclosure cages
A cage to keep out certain animals, usually predators, thus protecting the inhabitant.

Fauna
The animal life in a particular region or area at a certain time.

Flora
The plant life in a particular region or area at a certain time.

Flush
To drive the birds out of their cover.

Fodder crops
Crops that are planted to provide food for livestock.

Game cover crops
Crops that are planted to provide gamebirds with food and shelter. These are not harvested as a crop, but provide habitat for the gamebirds and other wildlife.

Hoppers
Feed containers usually steel or plastic barrels, usually filled with wheat, designed to allow easy access for gamebirds.

Hungry Gap
The period in late winter and early spring when food is very scarce for birds. During this time, supplementary food can be particularly important.

Improved grassland
Areas of grassland that have been improved for livestock, by grazing, mowing, sowing with desirable grass species, drainage or treatment with fertilizers or herbicides. Agricultural improvement usually results in decreased diversity of the grassland plants and dominance by a few quick-growing grasses.

Indicator species
A particular species that reflects the overall health of a wider group or species or an environment as a whole.

Invasive (non-native) species
A species that is not native to a particular ecosystem, and causes harm. They tend to reproduce quickly, and spread rapidly.

Invertebrate community
The range and mix of invertebrates found in a particular area.

Invertebrates
Invertebrates are animals that do not have a backbone. This includes a very wide variety of creatures, for example: insects, spiders, molluscs (snails, slugs, many sea creatures), crustaceans (crabs, lobsters etc), worms, jellyfish and many more.

IUCN
The International Union for Conservation of Nature and Natural Resources is the global authority on the status of the natural world and the measures needed to safeguard it.

Jinking
An unpredictable flight from side-to-side when flushed exhibited by certain birds such as woodcock.

Lead-in strips
Sections of cover crop planted to provide a channel of cover, and so avoid gamebirds using hedges as corridors to get to and from their release pens.

Marking birds
Watching where a shot bird lands to ensure it is found and retrieved as quickly as possible.

NE
Natural England. The government's adviser for the natural environment in England, helping to protect England's nature and landscapes for people to enjoy and for the services they provide.

NGC
National Gamebag Census, see chapter 10.

NGO
National Gamekeepers' Organisation:
www.nationalgamekeepers.org.uk

PCS
Partridge Count Scheme, see chapter 10.

Pesticides
Treatments to remove plant or animal pests – the term pesticides includes both herbicides, which kill groups of weeds, and insecticides, which kill groups of insects.

Picker-up
A person with a trained gundog retriever which locates and picks up game when it has been shot.

Poult
Young gamebirds. Pheasant poults are generally bought at 6-8 weeks old, and red-legged partridges at 11-13 weeks.

Raptors
Birds of prey. Raptors hunt and feed on rodents and other animals and include eagles, vultures, buzzards, kites, harriers, owls and others.

Release pen
Pheasants: A large, open-topped pen sited in woodland where pheasant poults are placed while they adapt to their environment. Partridge: Smaller, closed-topped pens, usually sited on open farmland, to hold partridges.

Residual grass
Grass that is left from the year before or dead grass that can provide good nesting cover for grey partridges.

Roding
The breeding display flight of woodcock, which is performed by the males between April and June. They fly over woodland at tree-top height with rapid wingbeats, whilst making a unique low, croaking call.

Roosting
A place where birds settle to sleep. Though it is widely perceived that birds roost in trees, as with pheasants, some birds roost on the ground, as with partridges, or on water, as with mallard.

Scrape
Scrapes are shallow depressions filled with water that are dug in fields to benefit wading birds and wildfowl.

Shelter belt
A line of trees or shrubs planted to protect an area, especially woodland, from wind and weather.

SSSI
Site of Special Scientific Interest, an area designated to protect a particular species or habitat.

Supplementary feed
Additional feed, usually grain, provided by the gamekeeper to supplement the food that gamebirds can forage for in the countryside.

Topping up
The practice of releasing additional birds throughout the season to replace those already shot.

Understorey
Plant life growing beneath the woodland canopy.

Unimproved habitat
Areas that have not been ploughed, sown, treated with pesticides, or had fertilizer spread.

Voluntary restraint
Shoots or Guns not shooting something that is a legal quarry species through their own choice, rather than being prevented from doing so by legislation.

Waders
A group of birds most of whom spend parts of their life wading in

the shallow waters of the sea, estuaries and lakes. They are referred to as "shorebirds" in America.

Wild bird mix
Seed mixes that include a range of species known to be attractive to, or provide good food resources for, wild birds. When sown as cover crops these can provide many benefits to farmland birds as well as gamebirds.

Appendix A - Shooting Seasons

The birds and animals shown in this table may be taken or killed as indicated. Dates are inclusive and apply to the whole of Great Britain unless otherwise stated.

Part 1 - Gamebirds

Grouse	12th August to 10th December
Ptarmigan	12th August to 10th December
Black game	20th August to 10th December
Partridge	1st September to 1st February
Pheasant	1st October to 1st February

Part 2 - Deer and other mammals

Red and Sika stags	England and Wales	1st August to 30th April
	Scotland	1st July to 20th October
Red and Sika hinds	England and Wales	1st November to 31st March
	Scotland	21st October to 15th February
Red/Sika hybrids		As for Red and Sika Deer
Fallow buck		1st August to 30th April
Fallow doe	England and Wales	1st November to 31st March
	Scotland	21st October to 15th February
Roe buck	England and Wales	1st April to 31st October
	Scotland	1st April to 20th October
Roe doe	England and Wales	1st November to 31st March
	Scotland	21st October to 31st March
Chinese Water Deer	England and Wales	1st November to 31st March
	Scotland	No close season
Muntjac		No close season
Hare	England and Wales	No close season
Mountain hare	Scotland	1st August to 28th/29th February
Brown hare	Scotland	1st October to 31st January
Rabbits		No close season

(See chapter 11 for further information on shooting ground game.)

Part 3 - Birds in Schedule 2 of the Wildlife and Countryside Act 1981 which may be killed or taken outside the close season and which may be sold dead from 1st September to 28th February.

Coot		1st September to 31st January
Common snipe		12th August to 31st January
Woodcock	England and Wales	1st October to 31st January
	Scotland	1st September to 31st January
Golden plover		1st September to 31st January

Tufted Duck	
Mallard	Above the high water mark of ordinary spring tides 1st September to 31st January.
Pintail	
Pochard	Below the high water mark of ordinary spring tides 1st September to 20th February
Shoveler	
Teal	
Wigeon	

The capercaillie which was formerly in this list is now protected in Scotland and is not ordinarily found in England and Wales. In England and Wales but no longer in Scotland it is customary to issue a general licence permitting the taking of mallard eggs up to 31st March for incubation in circumstances where the brood would have been unlikely to succeed in the wild. Note that whilst snipe may be shot in August they may not be sold dead until September.

Part 4 - Birds in Schedule 2 of the Wildlife and Countryside Act 1981 which may be killed or taken outside the close season but which may not be sold dead.

Canada goose	Above the high water mark of ordinary spring tides 1st September to 31st January.
Greylag goose	
Pink-footed goose	
White-fronted goose *(except in Scotland)*	Below the high water mark of ordinary spring tides 1st September to 20th February.
Gadwall	
Goldeneye	
Moorhen	1st September to 31st January

Due to the need to cull large numbers of feral greylag geese in parts of Scotland, such as Orkney and the Uists, licensing arrangements have been put in place to allow the local sale of goose meat. These licences allow the sale of goose meat in the areas covered by the pilot goose management culls but do not allow the sale of goose meat anywhere else. It is permissible to order goose meat and other products from these island-based retailers and have it sent to you.

Part 5 - Birds which may be shot or trapped at any time under general licence.

See **Quarry, predator and pest species** above for the broad terms of the licences, which may be viewed in detail on the BASC and relevant official websites. Licences are reviewed annually and it is essential you check at least once per year, preferably in early January, to ascertain the latest situation and to ensure that you are shooting within the terms of the relevant licence. In Scotland it is a requirement that you understand the terms of the licence before undertaking pest control. Please note this list is a summary of a fairly complicated licensing system. Some of the birds listed here may only be shot for a narrow range of reasons or at limited times, which is why reading the licence is essential.

In England, Scotland and Wales
Crow (Carrion and Hooded)
Magpie
Collared Dove Feral Pigeon
Rook
Jay
Woodpigeon
Jackdaw
Canada Goose
Ruddy Duck

Additionally in England
Egyptian Goose
Ring-necked Parakeet
Lesser Black-backed Gull
Monk Parakeet
Sacred Ibis
Indian House Crow

Additionally in Scotland
Great Black-backed Gull
Herring Gull
Lesser Black-backed Gull
Greylag goose

In Scotland if you control certain species, you are required to submit a return to SNH. Details are in the individual licences. SNH reserves the right to exclude the use of General Licence by "certain persons and/or on certain areas of land where there is evidence to suggest that a wild bird or birds have either been killed, injured or taken or where there has been an attempt to do so other than in accordance with a licence, or where General Licences are being misused". The ability to withdraw a general licence without there being any legal process or independent right of appeal is controversial.

Note that only woodpigeon may be sold dead. Other species may only be given away but see above for exceptions in respect of culled geese in Scotland.

The licences issued for shooting Ruddy Duck and Monk Parakeets are unique insofar as the intention is to eradicate the species in the wild, rather than to control them.

Gamekeepers, and others, in England and Wales who are troubled by Herring Gulls and Great Black-backed Gulls should apply for individual licences well before the damage is expected to happen. In Scotland Lesser Black-backed and Herring Gulls may only be shot for public health and similar reasons. Anyone needing to control them for other reasons must get an individual licence.

References

1. Draycott, RAH, Hoodless, AN & Sage, RB. (2008) Effects of pheasant management on vegetation and birds in lowland woodlands. *Journal of Applied Ecology*, **45**: 334–341

2. Sage, RB, Parish, DMB, Woodburn, MIA & Thompson, PGL. (2005) Songbirds using crops planted on farmland as cover for game birds. *European Journal of Wildlife Research*, **51**: 248–253

3. Parish, D & Sotherton, N. (2004) Game crops and threatened farmland songbirds in Scotland : a step towards halting population declines ? Bird Study, **51**: 107–112

4. Henderson, IG, Vickery, JA & Carter, N. (2004) The use of winter bird crops by farmland birds in lowland England. *Biological Conservation*, **118**: 21–32

5. Hoodless, AN & Draycott, RAH. (2005) Effects of pheasant management at wood edges. *GWCT Annual Review* **30**

6. Robertson, PA, Woodburn, MIA & Hill, DA. (1988) The effects of woodland management for pheasants on the abundance of butterflies in Dorset, England. *Biological Conservation*, **45**: 159–167

7. Davey, C. (University of Bristol, 2008). The impact of game management for pheasant (Phasianus colchicus) shooting on vertebrate biodiversity in British woodlands.

8. Sanchez-Garcia, C, Buner, FD & Aebischer, NJ. (2015) Supplementary winter food for gamebirds through feeders: Which species actually benefit? *Journal of Wildlife Management*, **79**: 832–845

9. GWCT. (2017). Guidelines for successful gamebird and songbird feeding.

10. Stoate, C & Szczur, J. (2001) Could game management have a role in the conservation of farmland passerines? A case study from a Leicestershire farm. Bird Study, **48**: 279–292

11. Stoate, C, Leake, A, Jarvis, P & Szczur, J. (2012). *Fields for the future.*

12. PACEC. (2014). *The Value of Sporting Shooting.*

13. Draycott, RAH, Hoodless, AN, Cooke, M & Sage, RB. (2012) The influence of pheasant releasing and associated management on farmland hedgerows and birds in England. *European Journal of Wildlife Research*, **58**: 227–234

14. Neumann, JL, Holloway, GJ, Sage, RB & Hoodless, AN. (2015) Releasing of pheasants for shooting in the UK alters woodland invertebrate communities. *Biological Conservation*, **191**: 50–59

15. Sage, RB & Swan, M. (2003). *Woodland conservation and pheasants.*

16. Sage, RB. (2007). *Guidelines for sustainable gamebird releasing.*

17. Sage, RB, Ludolf, C & Robertson, PA. (2005) The ground flora of ancient semi-natural woodlands in pheasant release pens in England. *Biological Conservation*, **122**: 243–252

18. Sage, RB, Woodburn, MIA, Draycott, RAH, Hoodless, AN & Clarke, S. (2009) The flora and structure of farmland hedges and hedgebanks near to pheasant release pens compared with other hedges. *Biological Conservation*, **142**: 1362–1369

19. Pressland, C. (University of Bristol, 2009). The impact of releasing pheasants for shooting on invertebrates in British woodlands.

20. Callegari, SE. (University of Reading, 2006). The impact of released

gamebirds on the nature conservation value of chalk grassland in central southern Britain.

21. Callegari, SE, Bonham, E, Hoodless, AN, Sage, RB & Holloway, GJ. (2014) Impact of game bird release on the Adonis blue butterfly Polyommatus bellargus (*Lepidoptera Lycaenidae*) on chalk grassland. *European Journal of Wildlife Research*, **60**: 781–787

22. Bicknell, J, Smart, J, Hoccom, DG, Amar, A, Evans, A, Walton, P & Knott, J. (2010). Impacts of non-native gamebird release in the UK: a review. *RSPB Research Report Number 40.*

23. Gilbert, J. (2007) National inventory of woodland and trees (1995-99): Analysis of Management and Biodiversity Data. *Forest Research*, Forestry Commission

24. Aebischer, N. (2017) How many birds are shot in the UK? *GWCT Annual Review*, 42–43

25. Sage, RB, Turner, CV., Woodburn, MIA, Hoodless, AN, Draycott, RAH & Sotherton, NW. (2018) Predation of released pheasants Phasianus colchicus on lowland farmland in the UK and the effect of predator control. *European Journal of Wildlife Research*, **64**: 14

26. Mayot, P. (2003) Repeuplement de faisans en été: volière à ciel ouvert ou petite volière de pré-lâcher? (Pheasant restocking in summer: English pen or small pre-releasing pen?). *Faune Sauvage*, **258**: 15–19.

27. Stoate, C. (2002) Multifunctional use of a natural resource on farmland: Wild pheasant (*Phasianus colchicus*) management and the conservation of farmland passerines. *Biodiversity and Conservation*, **11**: 561–573

28. Reynolds, JC, Stoate, C, Brockless, MH, Aebischer, NJ & Tapper, SC. (2010) The consequences of predator control for brown hares (*Lepus europaeus*) on UK farmland. *European Journal of Wildlife Research*, **56**: 541–549

29. Draycott, RAH, Hoodless, AN, Woodburn, MIA & Sage, RB. (2008) Nest predation of Common Pheasants Phasianus colchicus. *Ibis*, **150**: 37–44

30. Sage, RB, Putaala, A, Pradell-ruiz, V, Greenall, TL, Woodburn, MIA & Draycott, RAH. (2003) Incubation success of released hand-reared pheasants Phasianus colchicus compared with wild ones. *Wildlife Biology*, **9**: 179–184

31. Hill, D & Robertson, P. (1988) Breeding Success of Wild and Hand-Reared Ring-Necked Pheasants. *The Journal of Wildlife Management*, **52**: 446–450

32. Cramp, S, Simmons, K, Gillmour, R, Hollom, P, Hudson, R, Nicholson, E, Ogilvie, M, Olney, P, Roselaar, C, Voous, K, Wallace, D & Wattel, J. (Oxford University Press, 1980). *Handbook of the Birds of Europe, the Middle East and North Africa. The Birds of the Western Palearctic. Volume 2.*

33. Lever, C. (Hutchinson & Co, 1977). *The Naturalised Animals of the British Isles.*

34. Green, RE. (1984) Double nesting of the Red-legged Partridge Alectoris rufa. *Ibis*, **126**: 332–346

35. PACEC. (2006). *The Economic and Environmental Impact of Sporting Shooting.*

36. Anon. (1995). *Biodiversity: The UK Steering Group Report. Volume 2: Action Plans.*

37. Musgrove, A, Aebischer, N, Eaton, M, Hearn, R, Newson, S, Noble, D, Parsons, M, Risely, K & Stroud, D. (2013) Population estimates of birds in Great Britain and the United Kingdom. *British Birds*, **106**: 64–100

38. Sanchez-Garcïa, C, Perez, JA, Diez, C, Alonso, ME, Bartolome, DJ, Prieto, R, Tizado, EJ & Gaudioso, VR. (2017) Does targeted management work for red-legged partridges *Alectoris rufa*? Twelve years of the 'Finca de Matallana' demonstration project. *European Journal of Wildlife Research*, **63**: 24

39. Potts, G. (Collins, 2012). *Partridges. Countryside barometer. New Naturalist Library Book 121.*

40. Rands, MRW. (1988) The effect of nest site seleciton on nest predation in Grey Partridge *Perdix perdix* and Red-legged Partridge *Alectoris rufa*. *Ornis Scandinavica*, **19**: 35–40

41. Green, RE. (1984) The Feeding Ecology and Survival of Partridge Chicks (*Alectoris rufa* and *Perdix perdix*) on Arable Farmland in East Anglia. *The Journal of Applied Ecology*, **21**: 817

42. Potts, GR. (1978) The effects on a partridge population of predator control, insect shortages, different shooting pressures and releasing reared birds. *Game Conservancy Annual Review of 1977*, **9**: 75–83

43. Watson, M, Aebischer, NJ, Potts, GR & Ewald, JA. (2007) The relative effects of raptor predation and shooting on overwinter mortality of grey partridges in the United Kingdom. *Journal of Applied Ecology*, **44**: 972–982

44. Aebischer, NJ & Ewald, JA. (2010) Grey partridge Perdix perdix in the UK: Recovery status, set-aside and shooting. *Ibis*, **152**: 530–542

45. Potts, G. (1980) The effects of modern agriculture, nest predation and game management on the population ecology of partridges. *Advances in Ecological Research*, **11**: 1–82

46. Potts, GR. (Collins, 1986). *The Partridge. Pesticides, Predation and Conservation.*

47. Potts, G.R. & Aebischer, NJ. (Oxford University Press, 1991). Modelling the population dynamics of the grey partridge: conservation and management. in *Bird Population Studies: Their Relevance to Conservation and Management* (eds. Perrins, C. M., Lebreton, J. D. & Hirons, G. J. M.) 373–390

48. Massimino, D, Woodward, ID, Hammond, MJ, Harris, SJ, Leech, DI, Noble, DG, Walker, RH, Barimore, C, Dadam, D, Eglington, SM, Marchant, JH, Sullivan, MJP, Baillie, SR & Robinson, RA. (2017). *BirdTrends 2017: trends in numbers, breeding success and survival for UK breeding birds. Research Report 704.*

49. Connor, HE & Draycott, RAH. (2010) Management strategies to conserve the grey partridge: the effect on other farmland birds. *Aspects of Applied Biology*, **100**: 359–363

50. Dover, JW. (1997) Conservation headlands: Effects on butterfly distribution and behaviour. *Agriculture, Ecosystems and Environment*, **63**: 31–49

51. Dover, J, Sotherton, N & Gobbett, K. (1990) Reduced pesticide inputs on cereal field margins: the effects on butterfly abundance. *Ecological Entomology*, **15**: 17–24

52. Sotherton, NW. (1991). Conservation Headlands: a practical combination of intensive cereal farming and conservation. in *Ecology of Temperate Cereal Fields* 373–397

53. Ewald, J, Aebischer, N, Moreby, S & Potts, G. (2015) Changes in the cereal ecosystem on the South Downs of southern England, over the past 45 years. *Aspects of Applied Biology*, **128**: 11–19

54. Potts, G & Aebischer, N. (1995) Population dynamics of the grey partridge

Perdix perdix 1793–1993: monitoring, modelling and management. *Ibis*, **137**: S29–S37

55. Aebischer, N & Ewald, J. (2012) The grey partridge in the UK: population status, research, policy and prospects. *Animal Biodiversity and Conservation*, **35**: 353–362

56. Ewald, J, Wheatley, C, Aebischer, N, Moreby, S, Duffield, S, Crick, H & Morecroft, M. (2015) Influences of extreme weather, climate and pesticide use on invertebrates in cereal fields over 42 years. *Global Change Biology*, **21**: 3931–3950

57. Aebischer, NJ & Potts, GR. (1998) Spatial changes in grey partridge (*Perdix perdix*) distribution in relation to 25 years of changing agriculture in Sussex, U.K. *Gibier faune sauvage*, **15**: 293–308

58. Ewald, JA & Aebischer, NJ. (2000) Trends in pesticide use and efficacy during 26 years of changing agriculture in Southern England. *Environmental Monitoring and Assessment*, **64**: 493–529

59. Tapper, S. (1992). *Game Heritage.*

60. Aebischer, NJ, Davey, PD & Kingdon, NG. (2011) National Gamebag Census: Mammal Trends to 2009. Game and Wildlife Conservation Trust Available at: *https://www.gwct.org.uk/research/long-term-monitoring/national-gamebag-census/mammal-bags-comprehensive-overviews/fox/.*

61. Rands, M. (1986) Effect of hedgerow characteristics on partridge breeding densities. *Journal of Applied Ecology*, **23**: 479–487

62. Aebischer, NJ & Ewald, JA. (2004). Managing the UK grey partridge *Perdix perdix* recovery: Population change, reproduction, habitat and shooting. in *Ibis* **146**: 181–191

63. Rands, MRW. (1986) The survival of gamebird (*Galliformes*) chicks in relation to pesticide use on cereals. *Ibis*, **128**: 57–64

64. Tapper, SC, Potts, GR & Brockless, MH. (1996) The effect of an experimental reduction in predation pressure on the breeding success and population density of grey partridges *Perdix perdix*. *The Journal of Applied Ecology*, **33**: 965

65. Siriwardena, GM, Stevens, DK, Anderson, GQA, Vickery, JA, Calbrade, NA & Dodd, S. (2007) The effect of supplementary winter seed food on breeding populations of farmland birds: Evidence from two large-scale experiments. *Journal of Applied Ecology*, **44**: 920–932

66. Stoate, C. (2012) Filling the hungry gap - late-winter supplementary feeding of farmland birds. *Conservation Land Management* 10:4 p4

67. Parish, DMB & Sotherton, NW. (2007) The fate of released captive-reared grey partridges *Perdix perdix*: implications for reintroduction programmes. *Wildlife Biology*, **13**: 140–149

68. Buner, FD, Browne, SJ & Aebischer, NJ. (2011) Experimental assessment of release methods for the re-establishment of a red-listed galliform, the grey partridge (*Perdix perdix*). *Biological Conservation*, **144**: 593–601

69. Ewald, JA, Kingdon, NG & Santin-Janin, H. (2009). The GWCT Partridge Count Scheme: a volunteer-based monitoring and conservation promotion scheme. in *Gamebird 2006: Quail VI and Perdix XII* 27–37

70. Ewald, JA, Aebischer, NJ, Richardson, SM, Grice, P V. & Cooke, AI. (2010) The effect of agri-environment schemes on grey partridges at the farm level in England. *Agriculture, Ecosystems and Environment*, **138**: 55–63

71. Bence, SL, Stander, K & Griffiths, M. (2003) Habitat characteristics of harvest mouse nests on arable farmland. *Agriculture, Ecosystems & Environment*, **99**: 179–186

72. Parish, DMB & Sotherton, NW. (2008) Landscape-dependent use of a seed-rich habitat by farmland passerines: Relative importance of game cover crops in a grassland versus an arable region of Scotland. *Bird Study*, **55**: 118–123

73. Buner, FD, Brockless, MH & Aebischer, NJ. (2016) The rotherfield demonstration project. *The GWCT Annual Review*, 32–33

74. Draycott, RAH. (2012) Restoration of a sustainable wild grey partridge shoot in Eastern England. *Animal Biodiversity and Conservation*, **35**: 381–386

75. Ewald, J, Potts, G & Aebischer, N. (2012) Restoration of a wild grey partridge shoot: a major development in the Sussex study, UK. *Animal Biodiversity and Conservation*, **35**: 363–369

76. Southwood, T & Cross, D. (2002) Food Requirements of Grey Partridge *Perdix perdix* Chicks. *Wildlife Biology*, **8**: 175–183

77. Tillmann, J. (2009) Fear of the dark: night-time roosting and anti-predation behaviour in the grey partridge (*Perdix perdix L.*). *Behaviour*, **146**: 999–1023

78. Ford, J, Chitty, H & Middleton, AD. (1938) The food of Partridge chicks (*Perdix perdix*) in Great Britain. *The Journal of Animal Ecology*, **7**: 251–265

79. Rands, M. (1985) Pesticide Use on Cereals and the Survival of Grey Partridge Chicks: A Field Experiment. *Journal of Applied Ecology* **22**: 49–5449

80. Sotherton, NW, Robertson, PA & Dowell, SD. (1993). Manipulating pesticide use to increase the production of wild gamebirds in Britain. in *Quail III: National Quail Symposium* 92–101

81. Stoate, C, Henderson, IG & Parish, DMB. (2004). Development of an agri-environment scheme option: Seed-bearing crops for farmland birds. *Ibis* **146**: 203–209

82. Parish, D & Sotherton, N. (2004) Game crops as summer habitat for farmland songbirds in Scotland. *Agriculture, Ecosystems and Environment* **104**: 429–438

83. Stoate, C, Szczur, J & Aebischer, NJ. (2003) Winter use of wild bird cover crops by passerines on farmland in northeast England. *Bird Study*, **50**: 15–21

84. Newton, I. (William Collins, 2017). *Farming and Birds*.

85. Robertson, PA. (1992). Woodland Management for Pheasants. *Forestry commission bulletin 106.*

86. Staley, JT, Sparks, TH, Croxton, PJ, Baldock, KCR, Heard, MS, Hulmes, S, Hulmes, L, Peyton, J, Amy, SR & Pywell, RF. (2012) Long-term effects of hedgerow management policies on resource provision for wildlife. *Biological Conservation*, **145**: 24–29

87. Hinsley, S. & Bellamy, P. (2000) The influence of hedge structure, management and landscape context on the value of hedgerows to birds: A review. *Journal of Environmental Management*, **60**: 33–49

88. Walker, MP, Dover, JW, Sparks, TH & Hinsley, SA. (2006) Hedges and green lanes: Vegetation composition and structure. *Biodiversity and Conservation*, **15**: 2595–2610.

89. Kennedy, CEJ & Southwood, TRE. (1984) The Number of Species of Insects Associated with British Trees: A Re-Analysis. *The Journal of Animal Ecology*, **53**: 455-478

90. Dover, J & Sparks, T. (2000) A review of the ecology of butterflies in British

hedgerows. *Journal of Environmental Management*, **60**: 51-63

91.   Tillman, PG, Smith, HA & Holland, JM. (2012). Cover Crops and Related Methods for Enhancing Agricultural Biodiversity and Conservation Biocontrol: Successful Case Studies. in *Biodiversity and Insect Pests: Key Issues for Sustainable Management* 309–327

92.   Collins, KL, Boatman, ND, Wilcox, A, Holland, JM & Chaney, K. (2002) Influence of beetle banks on cereal aphid predation in winter wheat. *Agriculture, Ecosystems and Environment*, **93**: 337–350

93.   McCall, I. (1988). *Woodlands for Pheasants.*

94.   Forestry Commission. (2017). *Forestry Statistics 2017 Chapter 1: Woodland Areas and Planting.*

95.   Oldfield, TEE, Smith, RJ, Harrop, SR & Leader-Williams, N. (2003) Field sports and conservation in the United Kingdom. *Nature*, **423**: 531–3

96.   Duckworth, JC, Firbank, LG, Stuart, RC & Yamamoto, S. (2003) Changes in land cover and parcel size of British lowland woodlands over the last century in relation to game management. *Landscape Research*, **28**: 171–182

97.   Ferris, R & Carter, C. (2000). Maintaining Rides, Roadsides and Edge Habitats in Lowland Forests. *Forestry Commission bulletin 123.*

98.   Warren, M & Fuller, R. (1993). *Woodland rides and glade: their management for wildlife.*

99.   Fuller, RJ, Noble, DG, Smith, KW & Vanhinsbergh, D. (2005) Recent declines in populations of woodland birds in Britain: A review of possible causes. *British Birds* **98**: 116–143

100.   Mason, CF & Macdonald, SM. (2002) Responses of ground flora to coppice management in an English woodland - A study using permanent quadrats. *Biodiversity and Conservation*, **11**: 1773–1789

101.   Fuller, R & Warren, M. (1990). *Coppiced woodlands: their management for wildlife.*

102.   Siriwardena, GM, Calbrade, NA & Vickery, JA. (2008) Farmland birds and late winter food: Does seed supply fail to meet demand? *Ibis*, **150**: 585–595

103.   Robertson, P, Woodburn, M & Hill, D. (1993) Factors Affecting Winter Pheasant Density in British Woodlands. *Journal of Applied Ecology*, **30**: 459–464

104.   Robertson, PA, Woodburn, MIA, Neutel, W & Bealey, CE. (1993) Effects of Land-Use on Breeding Pheasant Density. *Journal of Applied Ecology*, **30**: 465–477

105.   Draycott, RAH, Woodburn, MIA, Carroll, JP & Sage, RB. (2005) Effects of spring supplementary feeding on population density and breeding success of released pheasants *Phasianus colchicus* in Britain. *Wildlife Biology*, **11**: 177–182

106.   Draycott, RAH, Hoodless, AN, Ludiman, MN & Robertson, PA. (1998) Effects of Spring Feeding on Body Condition of Captive-Reared Ring-Necked Pheasants in Great Britain. *The Journal of Wildlife Management*, **62**: 557

107.   Hoodless, AN, Draycott, RAH, Ludiman, MN & Robertson, PA. (1999) Effects of supplementary feeding on territoriality, breeding success and survival of pheasants. *Journal of Applied Ecology*, **36**: 147–156

108.   Fletcher, K, Aebischer, NJ, Baines, D, Foster, R & Hoodless, AN. (2010) Changes in breeding success and abundance of ground-nesting moorland birds in relation to the experimental deployment of legal predator control.

Journal of Applied Ecology, **47**: 263–272

109. Tharme, AP, Green, RE, Baines, D, Bainbridge, IP & O'Brien, M. (2001) The effect of management for red grouse shooting on the population density of breeding birds on heather-dominated moorland. *Journal of Applied Ecology*, **38**: 439–457

110. Robertson, PA. (1988) Survival of released pheasants, *Phasianus colchicus*, in Ireland. *Journal of Zoology*, **214**: 683–695

111. Rickenbach, O, Grüebler, MU, Schaub, M, Koller, A, Naef-Daenzer, B & Schifferli, L. (2011) Exclusion of ground predators improves Northern Lapwing Vanellus vanellus chick survival. *Ibis*, **153**: 531–542

112. White, PJC, Stoate, C, Szczur, J & Norris, K. (2008) Investigating the effects of predator removal and habitat management on nest success and breeding population size of a farmland passerine: A case study. *Ibis*, **150**: 178–190

113. White, PJC, Stoate, C, Szczur, J & Norris, K. (2014) Predator reduction with habitat management can improve songbird nest success. *Journal of Wildlife Management*, **78**: 402–412

114. Douglas, DJT, Bellamy, PE, Stephen, LS, Pearce-Higgins, JW, Wilson, JD & Grant, MC. (2014) Upland land use predicts population decline in a globally near-threatened wader. *Journal of Applied Ecology*, **51**: 194–203

115. Malpas, LR, Kennerley, RJ, Hirons, GJM, Sheldon, RD, Ausden, M, Gilbert, JC & Smart, J. (2013) The use of predator-exclusion fencing as a management tool improves the breeding success of waders on lowland wet grassland. *Journal for Nature Conservation*, **21**: 37–47

116. Isaksson, D, Wallander, J & Larsson, M. (2007) Managing predation on ground-nesting birds: The effectiveness of nest exclosures. *Biological Conservation*, **136**: 136–142

117. Cross, A, Perkins, A & Tompkins, D. (2016). *Curlew Country - Nest Monitoring Report Year 2.*

118. Petrovan, SO, Barrio, IC, Ward, AI & Wheeler, PM. (2011) Farming for pests? Local and landscape-scale effects of grassland management on rabbit densities. *European Journal of Wildlife Research*, **57**: 27–34

119. Morris, AJ & Gilroy, JJ. (2008) Close to the edge: Predation risks for two declining farmland passerines. *Ibis*, **150**: 168–177

120. Šálek, M, Kreisinger, J, Sedláček, F & Albrecht, T. (2009) Corridor vs. hayfield matrix use by mammalian predators in an agricultural landscape. Agriculture, *Ecosystems and Environment,* **134**: 8–13

121. Šálek, M, Kreisinger, J, Sedláček, F & Albrecht, T. (2010) Do prey densities determine preferences of mammalian predators for habitat edges in an agricultural landscape? *Landscape and Urban Planning*, **98**: 86–91

122. Roodbergen, M, van der Werf, B & Hotker, H. (2012) Revealing the contributions of reproduction and survival to the Europe-wide decline in meadow birds: Review and meta-analysis. *Journal of Ornithology* **153**: 53–74

123. Mustin, K, Arroyo, B, Beja, P, Newey, S, Irivine, RJ, Kestler, J & Redpath, SM. (2018) Consequences of game bird management for non-game species in Europe. *Journal of Applied Ecology*, **55**: 2285-2295

124. Reynolds, JC. (1990) Crow and magpie control: the use of call birds in cage traps. *The Game Conservancy Review*, **21**: 48–49

125. Tapper, SC, Swan, MC & Reynolds, JC. (1991) Larsen traps: a survey of members' results. *The Game Conservancy Review,* **22**: 82–86

126. Fokin, S & Blokhin, Y. (2013). Monitoring of the Woodcock population in European Russia (1996-2010). in *Seventh European Woodcock and Snipe Workshop* 29–35

127. Heward, CJ, Hoodless, AN, Conway, GJ, Nicholas, J, Gillings, S & Fuller, RJ. (2015) Current status and recent trend of the Eurasian Woodcock *Scolopax rusticola* as a breeding bird in Britain. *Bird Study*, 3657: 1–17

128. Lindström, Å, Green, M, Husby, M, Kålås, JA & Lehikoinen, A. (2015) Large-Scale Monitoring of Waders on Their Boreal and Arctic Breeding Grounds in Northern Europe. *Ardea*, 103: 3–15

129. Birdlife International. (2016) The IUCN Red List of Threatened Species. Available at: www.iucnredlist.org.

130. Eaton, M, Aebischer, N, Brown, A, Hearn, R, Lock, L, Musgrove, A, Noble, D, Stroud, D & Gregory, R. (2015) Birds of Conservation Concern 4: the population status of birds in the UK, Channel Islands and Isle on Man. *British Birds*, 108: 708–746

131. Hoodless, AN & Coulson, JC. (1994) Survival rates and movements of British and Continental Woodcock *Scolopax rusticola* in the British Isles. *Bird Study*, 41: 48–60

132. Heward, CJ, Hoodless, AN, Conway, GJ, Fuller, RJ, MacColl, AD & Aebischer, NJ. (2018) Factors affecting the distribution and abundance of Eurasian woodcock (*Scolopax rusticola*) breeding in Britain. *Journal of Ornithology*, 159: 955-965

133. Hoodless, A, Lang, D, Aebischer, N, Fuller, R & Ewald, J. (2009) Densities and population estimates of breeding Eurasian Woodcock *Scolopax rusticola* in Britain in 2003. *Bird Study*, 56: 15–25

134. Grant, MC, Orsman, C, Easton, J, Lodge, C, Smith, M, Thompson, G, Rodwell, S & Moore, N. (1999) Breeding success and causes of breeding failure of curlew *Numenius arquata* in Northern Ireland. *Journal of Applied Ecology*, 36: 59–74

135. Baines, D. (1990) The Roles of Predation, Food and Agricultural Practice in Determining the Breeding Success of the Lapwing (*Vanellus vanellus*) on Upland Grasslands. *The Journal of Animal Ecology*, 59: 915

136. Powell, A. (Oxford, 2012). Origins and non-breeding ecology of Eurasian woodcock.

137. Hoodless, A & Hirons, G. (2007) Habitat selection and foraging behaviour of breeding Eurasian Woodcock *Scolopax rusticola*: a comparison between contrasting landscapes. *Ibis*, 149: 234–249

138. Joint Nature Conservation Committee. (2015) Scheme to reduce disturbance to waterfowl during severe winter weather. Available at: http://jncc.defra.gov.uk/page-2894.

139. Sánchez-García, C, Williams, O & Hoodless, A. (2018) Regulation of body reserves in a hunted wader: implications for cold-weather shooting restrictions. *Journal of Applied Ecology*, 55: 2274-2284

140. Lehikoinen, A, Jaatinen, K, Vähätalo, A V., Clausen, P, Crowe, O, Deceuninck, B, Hearn, R, Holt, CA, Hornman, M, Keller, V, Nilsson, L, Langendoen, T, Tománková, I, Wahl, J & Fox, AD. (2013) Rapid climate driven shifts in wintering distributions of three common waterbird species. *Global Change Biology*, 19: 2071–2081

141. Wilson, AM, Ausden, M & Milsom, TP. (2004). Changes in breeding wader

populations on lowland wet grasslands in England and Wales: Causes and potential solutions. *Ibis* **146**: 32–40

142. The Game Conservancy. (1991). *Wildfowl management on inland waters. Green guide no. 3.*

143. Giles, N. (1992). *Wildlife after Gravel.*

144. Gaetke, LM, Chow-Johnson, HS & Chow, CK. (2014) Copper: toxicological relevance and mechanisms. *Archives of Toxicology*, **88**: 1929–1938

145. EFSA Panel on Contaminants in the Food Chain (CONTAM). (2010) Scientific Opinion on Lead in Food. *The European Food Safety Authority Journal*, **8**: 1570, 1–151

146. National Toxicology Programme. (2012). *NTP Monograph on health effects of low level lead.*

147. European Food Safety Authority. (2012) Lead dietary exposure in the European population. *EFSA Journal*, **10**: 2831

148. Food Standards Agency. (2012). Habits and behaviours of high-level consumers of lead-shot wild-game meat in Scotland. *Ref: J10106.*

149. Food Standards Agency. (2015) Advice to frequent eaters of game shot with lead. Available at: https://www.food.gov.uk/science/advice-to-frequent-eaters-of-game-shot-with-lead. (Accessed: 20th February 2018)

150. Iqbal, S, Blumenthal, W, Kennedy, C, Yip, FY, Pickard, S, Flanders, WD, Loringer, K, Kruger, K, Caldwell, KL & Jean Brown, M. (2009) Hunting with lead: association between blood lead levels and wild game consumption. *Environmental research*, **109**: 952–959

151. Tavecchia, G, Pradel, R, Lebreton, J-D, Johnson, AR & Mondain-Monval, J-Y. (2001) The effect of lead exposure on survival of adult mallards in the Camargue, southern France. *Journal of Applied Ecology*, **38**: 1197–1207

152. Pain, D, Cromie, R & Green, R. (2014). Poisoning of birds and other wildlife from ammunition-derived lead in the UK. in *Proceedings of the Oxford Lead Symposium* 58–84

153. (1999). *The Environmental Protection (Restriction on Use of Lead Shot) (England) Regulations 1999.*

154. Birkhead, M & Perrins, C. (1985) The breeding biology of the mute swan *Cygnus olor* on the River Thames with special reference to lead poisoning. *Biological Conservation*, **32**: 1–11

155. Potts, GR. (2005) Incidence of ingested lead gunshot in wild grey partridges (*Perdix perdix*) from the UK. *European Journal of Wildlife Research*, **51**: 31–34

156. Butler, D, Sage, R, Draycott, R, Carroll, J & Potts, GR. (2005) Lead exposure in ring-necked pheasants on shooting estates in Great Britain. *Wildlife Society Bulletin*, **33**: 583–589

157. Butler, D. (2005) Incidence of lead shot ingestion in red-legged partridges (*Alectoris rufa*) in Great Britain. *Veterinary Record*, **157**: 661

158. Kreager, N, Wainman, BC, Jayasinghe, RK & Tsuji, LJS. (2008) Lead pellet ingestion and liver-lead concentrations in upland game birds from southern Ontario, Canada. *Archives of Environmental Contamination and Toxicology*, **54**: 331–336

159. Scheuhammer, AM & Norris, SL. (1996) The ecotoxicology of lead shot and lead fishing weights. *Ecotoxicology* 5: 279–295

160. Pain, DJ, Amiard-Triquet, C, Bavoux, C, Burneleau, G, Eon, L & Nicolao-

Guillaumet, P. (1993) Lead poisoning in wild populations of Marsh Harriers *Circus aeruginosus* in the Camargue and Charente-Maritime, France. *Ibis*, **135**: 379–386

161. Pain, DJ, Bavoux, C & Burneleau, G. (1997) Seasonal blood lead concentrations in marsh harriers *Circus aeruginosus* from Charente-Maritime, France: Relationship with the hunting season. *Biological Conservation*, **81**: 1–7

162. Cromie, R, Loram, A & Harradine, J. (2010). *Compliance with the environmental protection (restriction on use of lead shot)(England) regulations 1999.*

163. Laulicht, F, Brocato, J, Cartularo, L, Vaughan, J, Wu, F, Kluz, T, Sun, H, Oksuz, BA, Shen, S, Paena, M, Medici, S, Zoroddu, MA & Costa, M. (2015) Tungsten-induced carcinogenesis in human bronchial epithelial cells. *Toxicology and Applied Pharmacology*, **288**: 33–39

164. Emond, CA, Vergara, VB, Lombardini, ED, Mog, SR & Kalinich, JF. (2015) Induction of Rhabdomyosarcoma by Embedded Military-Grade Tungsten/Nickel/Cobalt Not by Tungsten/Nickel/Iron in the B6C3F1 Mouse. *International Journal of Toxicology*, **34**: 44–54

165. Strigul, N, Koutsospyros, A, Arienti, P, Christodoulatos, C, Dermatas, D & Braida, W. (2005) Effects of tungsten on environmental systems. *Chemosphere*, **61**: 248–258

166. Jayasinghe, R, Tsuji, LJS, Gough, WA, Karagatzides, JD, Perera, D & Nieboer, E. (2004) Determining the background levels of bismuth in tissues of wild game birds: a first step in addressing the environmental consequences of using bismuth shotshells. *Environmental Pollution*, **132**: 13–20

167. Bush, K, Courvalin, P, Dantas, G, Davies, J, Eisenstein, B, Huovinen, P, Jacoby, GA, Kishony, R, Kreiswirth, BN, Kutter, E, Lerner, SA, Levy, S, Lewis, K, Lomovskaya, O, Miller, JH, Mobashery, S, Piddock, LJV, Projan, S, Thomas, CM, Tomasz, A, Tulkens, PM, Walsh, TR, Watson, JD, Witkowski, J, Witte, W, Wright, G, Yeh, P & Zgurskaya, HI. (2011) Tackling antibiotic resistance. *Nature Reviews Microbiology* **9**: 894–896

168. Borriello, S. (2017). *UK – Veterinary Antibiotic Resistance and Sales Surveillance Report 2016.*

169. ruma. (2017). *Targets Task Force Report.*

170. Robertson, GS, Aebischer, NJ & Baines, D. (2017) Using harvesting data to examine temporal and regional variation in red grouse abundance in the British uplands. *Wildlife Biology*, 2017:

171. Newey, S, Willebrand, T, Haydon, DT, Dahl, F, Aebischer, NJ, Smith, AA & Thirgood, SJ. (2007) Do mountain hare populations cycle? *Oikos*, **116**: 1547–1557

172. Aebischer, NJ. (Blackwell Publishing Ltd, 2009). Gamebird science, agricultural policy and biodiversity conservation in lowland areas of the UK. in *Recreational Hunting, Conservation and Rural Livelihoods - Science and Practice* (eds. Dickson, B., Hutton, J. & Adams, W. M.) 197–211

173. Tapper, S. (1999). *A Question of Balance.*

174. Aebischer, N.J.A. (2017). How many birds are shot in the UK? *GWCT Annual Review*, 42-43

GWCT Advisory Service

Get the best advice now

The GWCT's advisory team are the most experienced consultants in their field, able to provide advice and training across all aspects of game management, from wild bird production and farm conservation management to the effective and sustainable management of released game and compliance with the Code of Good Shooting Practice

Renowned for our science-based game and wildlife management advice that guarantees the best possible outcome from your shoot, we will work closely with your farm manager, gamekeeper and existing advisors to identify ways of making your game and shoot management more effective by providing tried and tested advice backed by science.

Services include:

- Best practice predation control techniques
- Sustainable management of released pheasants
- Grey partridge conservation
- Identifying farmland birds
- Managing woodland for butterflies, game and other wildlife
- The GWCT shoot biodiversity assessment service

Call us today on 01425 651013, email advisory@gwct.org.uk or visit www.gwct.org.uk/advisory

Join the GWCT

Make sure you never miss the latest news and events by joining the GWCT

As a member of the Trust you will not only be helping to fund the scientific research, you'll be the first to hear about it.

What you receive when you become a GWCT member:

- Priority access to dozens of unique courses and events taking place throughout the year.
- Free copies of *Gamewise*, our feature-packed magazine produced three times a year.
- Your own free personal copy of our
- annual Review.
- An invitation to the GWCT's Scottish Game Fair at Scone Palace.
- Regular email updates containing all our latest news and research findings.
- Membership of your local county group and invitations to events in your area.
- Pleasure from the knowledge that you're helping the British countryside thrive both now and in the future.

Call us today on 01425 652381 or visit www.gwct.org.uk/join